Divine Meditations

of

William Huntington

Divine Meditations

of

William Huntington

EDITED AND ABRIDGED BY
JOHN METCALFE

THE PUBLISHING TRUST
Church Road, Tylers Green, Penn, Buckinghamshire.

Printed and Published by
John Metcalfe Publishing Trust
Church Road, Tylers Green
Penn, Buckinghamshire

—

—

First Published 1991

—

ISBN 1 870039 24 6

—

Price £2.35

—

THE MINISTRY OF WILLIAM HUNTINGTON

THE Rev. William Romaine, Rector of St. Andrew Wardrobe and St. Ann's, Blackfriars, observed, 'God raises up such men as John Bunyan and William Huntington but once in a century.' John Sterling, the friend of Carlyle, says 'I remember a most scurrilous article of Southey's against Huntington, but his writings show him to be a worthy compeer of Bunyan and there is hardly anyone in history whose sincerity I could less easily doubt. His narrative is one of the most deeply affecting.'

Yet he was called 'a figure as lecherous as a Casanova or a mediaeval pope' in one cheap magazine, and 'an inferior quack' in another. The envious raged against him, and the wicked manufactured lies and slanders continually, calling him a liar, an adulterer, and so on, just as they did Bunyan and those before him. All their mire and froth came to nothing. The wicked fell. Huntington stands.

Among those who were prejudiced against Huntington was Thomas Burgess, afterwards minister at Deptford. 'I had heard many evil reports of that great man of God', said Burgess, 'and I thought he was a very awful character. However, I went to hear him. He set forth all my experience, from first to last, and my soul has been in union with him from that day to this.'

'Only those who heard Huntington preach', said the Rev. Samuel Adams, 'can have any idea of the greatness of his mind in spiritual things, or can ever feel what those felt who heard the glorious truths of the gospel from his own lips. I shall never forget the impression I received under the first sermon I heard from him. I could only weep and pray. I felt an inexpressible awe. His writings give but a faint idea of this truly wonderful and holy man. His power as a preacher was seldom equalled, never surpassed.'

Among his hearers were Sir William Hay; Sir Ludlow Harvey; Mr. Hannah, Comptroller of the Household to Princess Charlotte; Mr. Hunter, Keeper of the Observatory in Kew Gardens; Mr. Saunders, the King's State Coachman; Mr. Henry Peto, builder of London Bridge; and the Earl of Liverpool, afterwards Prime Minister, and several members of the royal household occasionally attended.

But, after all, the best testimony to Huntington's worth was the character and conduct of his regular hearers—of the thousands who thronged the chapels in Titchfield Street and Grays Inn Lane. William Stevens knew many of them, and he has left on record that their 'conversation was most spiritual and heavenly'. 'I have known many', he further observes, 'who in their last hours have blessed God for what he had done for their souls by Huntington's ministry. I never knew of one who did or could bear a contrary testimony.' Mr. Cleeve W. Hooper, writing in 1872, said he had listened to the 'edifying conversation of those godly people who used to attend Providence Chapel', and he could bear testimony that there were few at the time he was writing 'so spiritually minded, so richly taught.'

T.W.

CONTENTS

the first meditation

DIVINE MEDITATIONS

I

The First Meditation

I HAVE for some few weeks back been much indulged and helped by the Holy Spirit of promise, of whose influence, help, and energetic intercession at the throne of grace, I have been very watchful and observant; and, on the other hand, could not but wonder at the backwardness, deadness, dryness, and barrenness, both in power and in expression, when his sensible influence was withheld from me.

His divine Person, and his most benign influences and operations, were for many days my meditations, both by night and by day; and, during this time, these things were the principal subjects of my ministry; and, had I wrote them then, I have no doubt but thou wouldest have felt the blessed effects; but now it is not so with me; my harp is upon the willows and, with respect to sensible enjoyments, the Comforter that should relieve my soul seems to be far from me. Oh, what is all religion without the operation of the Holy Spirit! An empty show, and a weariness to the flesh.

I thought not a little of his divine personality; and wondered much how any man living, who reads the scriptures, could ever have the effrontery to deny his being a divine Person. But the world knows him not. 'I will send you a Comforter whom the world cannot receive, because it seeth him not, neither knoweth him; but ye know him, for he dwelleth with you, and shall be in you.' He is therefore to be known by all believers: and those who do know him will glorify him and honour him; reverence him and adore him; and we know that all who are destitute of him, and strangers to his operations, are sensual men, and know nothing but what they know naturally.

Hence some have called the Holy Spirit no more than a quality, or an attribute of God; others an influence only; others no more than a name; avowing that there is but one Person in the Godhead, but a plurality of names: as some heretics give it out. But we know that no curious diving, no speculative prying, no presumptuous intruding, will meet with the divine approbation. 'God resisteth the proud.' But O how safe, how sweet, how salutary, how satisfactory, how humbling and softening, are the sweet influences, operations, discoveries, and communi cations, of the Holy Spirit upon the souls of the children of God!

Various things are meant by the word 'spirit' in the holy scriptures: as wind, the spirit of beasts, and the souls of men, and angels, both good and bad. But the Holy Ghost is distinguished from all these, being emphatically called God, not in a figurative or metaphoric, but in an absolute sense; 'to the acknowledgement of the mystery of God, and of the Father, and of Christ', Col. 2:2. In which passage the Holy Ghost stands first in the Holy Trinity, and he is distinct from the Father and from Christ: and surely, if he were not essentially God, to all intents and purposes, he never would have inspired the apostle to name and place him as God before the Father.

The church also is called 'the temple of the Holy Ghost; as God hath said, I will dwell in them and walk in them.' No spirit whatever, that is mentioned in all the book of God, is ever numbered with the Persons in the Holy Trinity, or ranked with the Father and the Son, except the Holy Ghost. Nor is the church the property, the temple, or the habitation, of any but of God alone: and, as the church is called the temple of the Holy Ghost, the Holy Ghost must be God.

A ghost is a spirit. The Holy Ghost and the Holy Spirit is one and the same in the original, as say the learned. Now what I have upon my mind, in writing this meditation, is upon this important subject: and, however weakly, or however imperfectly I may express myself, I am fully persuaded, by my own experience, that it is most safe, and ever will be satisfactory and establishing to the elect of God, who are regenerated and renewed by the Holy Spirit, to believe as I do: while the contrary is most dangerous, if not perilous: I mean, that the Holy Ghost must be acknowledged to be a divine Person by all those who are sanctified, and who hope to be saved.

They must acknowledge the mystery of God, of the Father, and of Christ; for we are baptized in the name of all the Three, and therefore, in our holy profession, we must acknowledge this greatest mystery of all mysteries.

A person, according to the account of learned men, is an individual being, an intelligent agent, who is singular, and subsists, lives, speaks, understands, acts, and works; and such is the Holy Ghost.

Nor is there a distinct personal character but what the holy scriptures apply to him; such as I, me, him, he, his, thou. As for instance, 'Separate me Barnabas and Saul for the work whereunto I have called them.' 'And when he is come he shall guide you into all truth.' Again, 'I will send you a Comforter, whom the world cannot receive, because it seeth him not, neither knoweth him; but ye know him, for he dwelleth with you, and shall be in you.' Again, 'Is the Spirit of the Lord straitened? Are these his doings?' Again, 'Whither shall I go from thy Spirit, or whither shall I flee from thy presence? If I go up into heaven, thou art there.'

Sure I am that these personal characters cannot be applied to a name or to a quality in God, or to an influence from him, or to an accident, or to a transient impression; much less to a non-entity. It is true, that personal characters, and personal actions, are sometimes ascribed to things inanimate; as, The trees went forth to choose themselves a king, and invited the vine and the olive to reign over them, who refused; and the bramble bid them put themselves under his shadow, Judges 9:8-15. The Red Sea also is represented as seeing and fleeing. 'Let the floods clap their hands: let the hills be joyful together.' Yet we have no voice from any of these, only dumb signs at best; these all wanted persons to speak for them. Jotham speaks for the trees and the bramble: Habakkuk speaks the motions of the sea, and David the actions of the little hills.

But the Holy Spirit wants none to speak for him; he can speak of himself, and for himself. He spoke in Adam, giving names to all creatures. He spoke to Philip; 'Go near and join thyself to this chariot.' He spoke to Peter; 'The Spirit said unto him, Behold, three men seek thee; arise therefore, and get thee down, and go with them, nothing doubting.' The Spirit said, 'Separate me Barnabas and Saul.' 'Blessed are the dead which die in the Lord: Yea, saith the Spirit, that they may rest from their labours, and their works do follow them.'

The Holy Spirit not only speaks; but all that have ever spoken to any good purpose have been taught to speak by him; he brings the things to their minds, puts words in their mouths, and teaches them how to pronounce them. 'Which things also we speak, not in the words which man's wisdom teacheth, but which the Holy Ghost teacheth', I Cor. 2:13. The Spirit put a word in Balaam's mouth, and bade him speak thus and thus; and the apostles spake as the Spirit gave them utterance.

He not only speaks to the saints, and in them, but he teaches us in some measure to discern between those whom he teaches to speak, and those who follow their own spirit, and speak a vision out of their own heart, and not out of the mouth of the Lord.

And how evident this is in all who write or speak of divine things without the Spirit's teaching! What flagrant errors, self-contradictions, inconsistencies, confusion, and darkening of counsel, doth appear! Instead of making rough places plain, and crooked things straight, they make the plainest places rough, and the straightest things crooked; and, instead of going through the gates, and removing the stumblingblocks, and casting up the highway, they grope like the blind for the wall, cause many to stumble at the law, and destroy the way of our paths.

And if at any time any of them appear to be tolerably sound in the letter, yet the deep things of the text, the unctuous matter of it, or the choice experience of the holy penmen, that lies hid in it, is never dived into, nor brought up; the glorious beauty of it is obscured, the surface of it is skimmed over; a few parallel texts are brought in, and dark constructions put upon the words, and the passage left more obscure than when the workman began.

There is nothing in your ears but swelling words and empty sound; and nothing in your soul but leanness and beggary. Instead of watering the trees of righteousness, or refreshing the bowels of the saints, these clouds without rain rather exhale or dry up all the dew of heaven that is on the soul, however refreshed before. Such workmen obscure and becloud the Spirit's work, cast a dimness on the brightest evidences, contract the most enlarged heart, and imprison those whom the Lord has made free indeed. This I know by woeful experience. And it must be so; for, 'The natural man discerneth not the things of the Spirit of God, nor can he know them, because they are spiritually discerned.'

Personal properties also, or those properties and things which are ascribed to persons, are also ascribed to the Holy Spirit; such as will, power, mind, judgment, wisdom, understanding, knowledge, love, joy, grief, vexation, for instance; 'All these worketh that one and the self-same Spirit, dividing to every man severally as he will.' 'Mighty signs and wonders by the power of the Holy Ghost.' 'And God that searcheth the heart knoweth what is the mind of the spirit.' And, 'The Lord of hosts shall be for a Spirit of judgment to him that sitteth in judgment': 'Upon him shall rest the Spirit of wisdom and understanding, the Spirit of counsel and might, the Spirit of knowledge and of the fear of the Lord.' Again, 'Now I beseech you, for the Lord Jesus Christ's sake, and for the love of the Spirit.' Again, 'You received the word with joy of the Holy Ghost.' 'Grieve not the Spirit of God, by which ye are sealed.' 'But they rebelled and vexed his Holy Spirit till he turned to be their enemy, and fought against them.'

I cannot see how all the above-mentioned things can with propriety be ascribed to anything but a person. To apply them to a quality, an accident, a name, or a nonentity, must be absurd to the last degree.

And I have often thought that, if men were allowed to take the same liberties with the evidences of a purchase, a man's will and testament, title-deeds, and writings of estates, that some take with the word of God, there are lawyers and counsellors wise enough to dispute every landholder in the nation out of all that he hath, and even out of his own personality and existence too.

For it is but to prove that there is no such man, no such person; that it is only a name; and all the relative or personal characters are to be understood in a figurative or an allegorical sense; and that it means no more than a quality in man, or a power put forth by man on certain occasions; or that it signifies only the breath of a man's mouth, an accident, or a transient emanation, flowing out with his words when he speaks. Allow a wise lawyer or counsellor to go this way to work, and we should soon see the greatest landholders in the nation begging in the streets.

the second meditation

II

The Second Meditation

I SHALL now mention some few works and actions which the scriptures ascribe to the Spirit, and which are personal works and actions, such as none but real persons can do.

None but persons can bear record to the truth of any contract, covenant, or agreement; nor be admitted as a witness in such cases, or to any deed, or upon any trial whatever. But, 'There are three that bear record in heaven; the Father, the Word, and the Holy Ghost: and there are three that bear witness on earth; the Spirit, the water, and the blood.' 'And we are witnesses of these things', says the apostle; 'and so is also the Holy Ghost; whom God hath given to them that obey him', Acts 5:32.

The Spirit bears witness to the truth of the word; he gives testimony to the word of his grace, and to the truth of their commission whom he sends to preach it. He brings the righteousness of Christ to the soul; 'We are justified in the name of the Lord Jesus, and by the Spirit of our God.' And he bears witness to our justification, and to our adoption. 'He that believeth hath the witness in himself.' And even in the court of a believer's conscience his witness is so powerful and effectual, that neither law, devil, nor sin, which is represented as crying to heaven: no, nor even conscience itself, is suffered to speak.

And this witness is true, and is no lie; and we are to abide in him. I know that Jacob set up a pillar in Bethel, and that Laban and Jacob gathered an heap of stones together at mount Gilead, and called them witnesses; but these were only to help the treacherous memory of persons, who are apt to forget, as Jacob did, when God bid him arise, and go up to Bethel, where he anointed the pillar.

Power and authority qualifying, equipping, and investing men with offices, must be personal works. 'You shall receive power after that the Holy Ghost is come upon you.' 'To one is given the word of wisdom, to another faith, to another divers kinds of tongues, to another the interpretation of tongues; and all these worketh that one and the self-same spirit.' 'Take heed to yourselves, and to the flock over which the Holy Ghost hath made you overseers', Acts 20:28. And, 'As they ministered to the Lord, and fasted, the Holy Ghost said, Separate me Barnabas and Saul for the work whereunto I have called them. So they being sent forth by the Holy Ghost departed', Acts 13:2,4. 'And they were forbidden to preach the word in Asia.' 'And they assayed to go into Bithynia, but the Spirit suffered them not.'

Now upon the whole, if speaking, teaching, leading; qualifying of men with grace, gifts, and abilities for the ministerial work; furnishing them with wisdom and knowledge, and giving them divers kinds of tongues; appointing them to the office of overseers, and telling them what to say; giving readiness of mind, aptitude and utterance in speaking; telling them where to go, and forbidding them to go here and there, where he had no work for them to do, at least not at that season; if these are not personal works and actions, what are?

There are some, I believe, in the world, who deny the very being of a God; 'The fool hath said in his heart, There is no

God.' These must be left to be convinced by the torments of the damned. But I believe there are very few, who profess to believe the bible, but will allow that there is one divine Person in the Godhead, which is in general allowed to be God the Father; though many will not allow the Saviour to be a Person, although he is his only-begotten Son, the Son of the Father in truth and love: and still less will they allow divine personality to the Holy Ghost; though the scriptures ascribe the same personal characters, properties, works, and actions, to the Son, and to the Spirit, as they do to God the Father.

Therefore, if the Father be a Person, the Son and Spirit must. The work of creation is ascribed to the Holy Ghost, as well as to the Son and to the Father: 'The Spirit of God moved upon the face of the waters.' He operated upon the confused chaos, and brought it into beautiful order. 'By his Spirit he hath garnished the heavens, his hand hath formed the crooked serpent', Job 26:13. 'By the Word of the LORD were the heavens made, and all the host of them by the breath of his mouth', Psalm 33:6. Here the creation of the heavens is ascribed to the essential Word, and to the Holy Spirit. 'Thou sendest forth thy Spirit, they are created, and thou renewest the face of the earth.' Here is the work of creation ascribed to the Spirit, and it is he that renews the face of the earth every spring. The creation of man is ascribed to the Holy Spirit also. 'The Spirit of God hath made me, and the breath of the Almighty hath given me life', Job 33:4.

Nor was the Holy Spirit a spectator when Christ appeared for our salvation. It was the Holy Ghost that came upon the Virgin Mary at her conception, and that formed the human nature which Christ assumed, and preserved it from every stain or spot of original sin, and then rested upon him with all his fulness of gifts and grace. He applied the word which the

Saviour spoke, and displayed his power in the miracles that he wrought; and those that blasphemed either his words or his power, blasphemed against the Holy Ghost. It was through the eternal Spirit that he offered himself in sacrifice to God, and it was the same Spirit that quickened our Lord's body in the tomb. 'He was put to death in the flesh, but quickened by the Spirit.'

And under his great power the apostles gave witness of the resurrection of the Lord Jesus; and hence it is said that he is declared to be the Son of God with power, according to the testimony of the Spirit of holiness, by the resurrection from the dead, Rom. 1:4.

Making the saints meet for heaven lies much upon the Holy Ghost. It is he that applies the word, and makes it effectual: the word comes in power and in the Holy Ghost; he convinces of sin; and it is the Spirit that quickens the dead sinner; and, as a Spirit of illumination and understanding, he enlightens him, testifies of Christ to him, works faith in him to believe, regenerates and renews him; takes the Lord's righteousness and peace, and shows them to the sinner; works the life and power of reigning grace in him, and sets up the kingdom of God in the heart, which stands in power, in righteousness, and peace, and joy in the Holy Ghost.

The law of faith by the Saviour, which the isles were to wait for, is applied and made effectual by the Holy Ghost, who is our last lawgiver. 'The law of the Spirit of life in Christ Jesus hath made me free from the law of sin and death.'

He bears witness to our adoption, and empowers us to claim it; produces the firstfruits of glory in our hearts, which are called the firstfruits of the Spirit; and is the pledge and earnest of the future inheritance. He seals us up to the day of redemption; renews us, or restores the lost image of God to us, and sanctifies us, and carries on his sanctifying, renewing, and transforming work in us, and makes us meet for the inheritance with the saints in light: 'That the offering up of the Gentiles may be accepted, being sanctified by the Holy Ghost.'

Sins against the Holy Spirit, in his work and operations, are taken notice of in a very particular manner, and are highly resented, even in the saints, and are punished with peculiar severity in the daring and presumptuous. The Israelites in the wilderness vexed his Holy Spirit, till he turned to be their enemy, and fought against them. Some of the young Gentile converts grieved him, and many were sickly and weak among them, and many slept, for their unbecoming behaviour at the Lord's table.

The Holy Spirit, says Christ, shall glorify me. And the Spirit is grieved when the Lord is dishonoured. Ananias and Sapphira, agreeing together in sin, tempted the Spirit of the Lord, and Satan filled their hearts to lie to the Holy Ghost. 'Thou hast not lied unto men, but unto God', says Peter, Acts 5. Therefore the Holy Ghost is God. And they were both struck dead upon the spot for it.

Great and innumerable sins against God in his law, as in Manasseh and others, have been forgiven; and many awful things done and spoken against the Son of man have been pardoned, as may be seen in Paul. But those that do despite to the Spirit of grace; who willingly and wilfully counteract his operations and designs in the souls of God's people; and who see his power, and yet oppose, hate, and fight against it; and who ridicule and blaspheme both the author and his operations; never have been, nor ever will be forgiven; for the sin against the Holy Ghost shall not be forgiven unto men, Mt. 12:31.

And can any man in his senses believe, or attempt to affirm, that the all-wise God, the Judge of all the earth, who is rich in mercy and abundant in goodness and in truth, would exclude men from all possibility of pardon, and doom them to eternal damnation, for sinning against a name, an accident, or only a quality, attribute, perfection, or a power in God, which may be transiently put forth, and displayed as an operation on man? Surely sinning against God the Father himself, which is sinning against all the revealed perfections and attributes of his nature, must be a more heinous crime than sinning against a single quality in him.

And yet all manner of sins and blasphemies, committed against him in the law, have been forgiven unto men; but the blasphemy against the Holy Ghost never was nor ever will be. And why this sin unto death should be emphatically called the great transgression, I cannot conceive, if the Holy Ghost, against whom it is committed, be not the great and terrible God.

The dispensation of the gospel, in the administration of it, is peculiarly his: hence it is called the ministration of the Spirit, that exceeds the former ministration in glory, II Cor. 3:8. He is the operator and worker of all good from God, through Christ in men; and of all the glory and praise that redounds to God by men; and will be greatly concerned in the first resurrection, the resurrection of the just. 'The dead shall hear the voice of the Son of God'; and the Spirit will attend it, and quicken them all, as it is written; 'But, if the Spirit of him that raised up Jesus from the dead dwell in you, he that raised up Christ from the dead shall also quicken your mortal bodies, by his Spirit that dwelleth in you', Rom. 8:11.

the third meditation

III

The Third Meditation

THAT the Holy Spirit is properly a Person, I have endeavoured to prove from scripture; and that he is a divine Person appears as plain, because he personally subsists and has life in himself. 'As the Father hath life in himself, so hath he given to the Son to have life in himself', John 5:26. And so hath the Spirit life in himself.

This appears in his creation-work. 'The Spirit of God hath made me, and the breath of the Almighty hath given me life', Job 33:4. He quickened, animated, and inspired Adam, and furnished him with a life of love. What power but a divine Person, who has life in himself, could form a living soul in Adam, and give him life, righteousness, and true holiness? He is the author of natural and spiritual life. 'It is the Spirit that quickeneth.' And, as he giveth spiritual life, so he maintains it; hence he is called, 'A well of living water, springing up into everlasting life', John 4:14.

And all the elect of God, who are by nature dead in trespasses and sins, and children of wrath, even as others, these doth the Holy Spirit quicken. I will put my Spirit in you, and ye shall live, Ezekiel 37:14. Hence our Saviour says, 'If any man thirst, let him come unto me, and drink. He that believeth on me, as the scripture hath said, out of his belly shall flow rivers of living water. But this spake he of the Spirit, which they that believe on him shall receive; for the Holy Ghost was not yet given, because that Jesus was not yet glorified.' It was the Spirit that quickened the Saviour's body in the tomb. He was put to death in the flesh, but quickened by the Spirit, I Peter 3:18.

Hence the Spirit is expressly called life; and he will, at the last day, quicken all that ever died in the Lord. 'And, if Christ be in you, the body is dead because of sin; but the Spirit is life because of righteousness.' I have sowed and you have reaped; 'And he that reapeth receiveth wages, and gathereth fruit unto life eternal; that both he that soweth and he that reapeth may rejoice together', John 4:36. The Spirit, as a well of living water, shall spring up into everlasting life.

This is the glorious harvest promised, as the present is the seedtime, in which the blessed crop that we have already got in hope is sown; for, 'He that soweth to the Spirit, shall of the Spirit reap life everlasting', Gal. 6:8. If, therefore, the Spirit be not a Person, and a divine Person too, who has eternal life in himself, we never could reap everlasting life from him by yielding spiritual obedience to him. I say spiritual obedience, because we are said to serve in newness of Spirit, and not in the oldness of the letter, which is only bodily exercise. And we are said, likewise, to worship God in the Spirit, and to walk in newness of life.

Furthermore, the names which, in the strictest sense, are peculiar to God, are by the scriptures given to the Holy Ghost. As Jehovah; which is an incommunicable name of God. 'Thou, whose name alone is Jehovah, art the most high over all the earth', Psalm 83:18. He, whom the children of Israel tempted and proved, vexed and rebelled against, was Jehovah. And Isaiah ascribes it to the Holy Ghost; 'But they rebelled, and vexed his Holy Spirit: therefore he was turned to be their enemy, and fought against them', Isaiah 63:10.

The apostle ascribes the same to him. 'Wherefore, as the Holy Ghost saith, Today, if ye will hear his voice, harden not your hearts, as in the provocation, in the day of temptation in the wilderness; when your fathers tempted me, proved me, and saw my works forty years. Wherefore I was grieved with that generation, and said, They do always err in their heart; and they have not known my ways. So I sware in my wrath, they shall not enter into my rest.'

Isaiah and the author of the Epistle to the Hebrews, ascribe this tempting and rebelling of the Israelites to be done against the Holy Ghost; therefore the Holy Ghost must be Jehovah, and so it is written, 'And he called the name of the place Massah, and Meribah, because of the chiding of the children of Israel, and because they tempted Jehovah, saying, Is Jehovah among us or not?' Exodus 17:7. It is therefore plain that the Holy Ghost is Jehovah, which incommunicable name is peculiar to the Most High God.

The Holy Ghost is called God, not in a figurative, but in a proper sense. 'Know ye not that ye are the temple of God, and the Spirit of God dwelleth in you?' I Cor. 3:16. What is not essentially God cannot be the Spirit of God; therefore the Holy Ghost is God. The Spirit of Jehovah is Jehovah the Spirit; the Spirit of God is God the Spirit. And this rule may be seen in the Epistle to the Corinthians. 'Nevertheless, when it shall turn to the Lord, the veil shall be taken away. Now the Lord is that Spirit; and where the Spirit of the Lord is there is liberty.' The Spirit of the Lord is the Lord the Spirit. Hence we may safely conclude that the Holy Ghost is Jehovah, God, and Lord.

And to show the divine equality of the adorable Persons in the Godhead, each Person at times is named or placed first. Sometimes Christ is named first. 'The grace of the Lord Jesus Christ, and the love of God, and the communion of the Holy Ghost, be with you all. Amen.' Sometimes the Holy Spirit stands first. 'That their hearts might be comforted, being knit together in love, and unto all riches in the full assurance of understanding; to the acknowledgement of the mystery of God, and of the Father, and of Christ.' Sometimes God the Father stands first. 'For there are three that bear record in heaven; the Father, the Word, and the Holy Ghost: and these three are one.'

Now, as this last order is not always attended to, it shows that one is not before or after another; and that one is not greater or less than the other.

Again; 'Now, there are diversities of gifts, but the same Spirit; and there are differences of administrations, but the same Lord; and there are diversities of operations, but it is the same God, which worketh all in all', I Cor. 12:4-6. Here the Holy Ghost takes the name of Spirit, Lord, and God, to himself; and therefore he must be the Spirit, Lord, and God. Sometimes the Holy Ghost is prayed to as God. 'But the Lord is faithful, who shall establish you, and keep you from evil. And we have confidence in the Lord touching you, that ye both do and will do the things which we command you. And the Lord direct your hearts into the love of God, and into a patient waiting for Christ.'

The Lord, who is faithful, and who stablishes the churches, and keeps them from evil, and in whom Paul places his confidence, is the Holy Ghost; and he is prayed to, that he may direct the saints' hearts into the love of God, and into the patient waiting for Christ. The Holy Spirit is prayed to as a divine Person, to direct souls into the love of God, who is another Person; and into the patient waiting for Christ, which is another, and a distinct Person from the former two.

That the Holy Ghost is truly and essentially God appears from the scriptures, which ascribe divine attributes and perfections to him; such as eternity. 'Through the eternal Spirit he offered himself to God', Heb. 9:14. Omniscience also. 'The Spirit searcheth all things, yea, the deep things of God: for what man knoweth the things of a man, save the spirit of man which is in him? even so the things of God knoweth no man, but the Spirit of God', I Cor. 2:10,11.

Omnipotence is ascribed to him. 'The Holy Ghost shall come upon thee, and the power of the Highest shall overshadow thee', Luke 1:35. He is called the Spirit of counsel and might, Isaiah 11:2. And the Spirit of power and of a sound mind, II Tim. 1:7. How can he be called the Spirit of power, the Spirit of might, and the power of the Highest, if he be not the Almighty God? Nothing can be the power of the Highest but omnipotence itself; and whatever is omnipotent is God.

Omnipresence. 'Whither shall I go from thy Spirit? or whither shall I flee from thy presence? If I ascend up into heaven, thou art there: If I make my bed in hell, behold, thou art there. If I take the wings of the morning, and dwell in the uttermost parts of the sea; even there shall thy hand lead me, and thy right hand shall hold me', Psalm 139:7-10. Here is the Holy Spirit, and his presence, and his hand, in all places; therefore he must be omnipresent, and immensity itself, seeing there is no going from him, either in heaven or in earth, in the sea or in hell.

Holiness also. He is declared to be the Son of God with power, according to the Spirit of holiness, by the resurrection from the dead, Rom. 1:4. If he be the Spirit of holiness he must have holiness in himself, as he has; and he is the author of holiness in all the saints, for they are sanctified by the Holy Ghost, who dwells in them. 'Know ye not that your bodies are the temples of the Holy Ghost?' 'Ye are the temple of the living God; as God hath said, I will dwell in them, and walk in them; and I will be their God, and they shall be my people', II Cor. 6:16.

He is called the Spirit of truth, and truth itself, who leads the saints into all truth. The Spirit of wisdom also; and, if he be the Spirit of truth, and truth itself, then he must be divine verity and divine wisdom. All these things, properly considered, are sufficient to prove that the Holy Ghost is a Person, a divine Person, and therefore truly and properly God.

the fourth meditation

IV

The Fourth Meditation

SINCE concluding the last meditation, my head and my heart have been conceiving and bringing forth again, insomuch that I think I have more oil in my cruse now than when I began. My horn is exalted like the horn of an unicorn, and I am anointed with fresh oil, Psalm 92:10. Therefore I will proceed to show that the Holy Ghost is a distinct Person. He is said to proceed from the Father. 'When the Comforter is come, whom I will send unto you from the Father, even the Spirit of truth, which proceedeth from the Father, he shall testify of me', John 15:26. If he proceed from the Father, he must be distinct from him from whom he proceeds.

Again; 'It is expedient for you that I go away: for if I go not away, the Comforter will not come unto you; but if I depart, I will send him.' Here the Spirit proceeds from the Son also, as well as from the Father. And, as he is distinct from the Father, so he is also from the Son; 'I will send him.'

The Spirit, which is sent, is a distinct Person from him that sends him. He is likewise called another. 'I will pray the Father, and he shall give you another Comforter.' God is called the Father of mercies, and the God of all comfort: the Saviour is called the consolation of Israel, which good old Simeon waited to see; and Christ, being about to leave his flock, promises to send them another Comforter, that should abide with them for ever; and if he be another Comforter, he must be distinct both from the Father and the Son, or else he cannot be another, but must be the same.

I believe that God the Father never did any works from which the Son or the Spirit were excluded. 'Verily, verily, I say unto you, the Son can do nothing of himself, but what he seeth the Father do: for what things soever he doeth, these also doeth the Son likewise', John 5:19. Nor did he ever work any work from which the Spirit was excluded. Their distinct personality appears in all their divine operations; and in every work they seem to be jointly concerned. In the secret councils of old, and in the decree of election, and in the covenant of grace which was made from everlasting, they were jointly concerned: there was the Father choosing, the Son in whom the choice was made undertaking to save, and the Spirit to sanctify and make obedient the objects chosen. 'Elect according to the foreknowledge of God the Father, through sanctification of the Spirit unto obedience, and sprinkling of the blood of Jesus Christ', I Peter 1:2.

This will appear more plain in the following passage, where you have an account of the covenant, and of the Persons in the Holy Trinity altogether. 'As for me, this is my covenant with them, saith the Lord, My Spirit that is upon thee, and my words which I have put in thy mouth, shall not depart out of thy mouth, nor out of the mouth of thy seed, nor out of the mouth of thy seed's seed, saith the Lord, from henceforth and for ever', Isa. 59:21. Here is the Father and the Son agreeing about a covenant; 'I have made a covenant with my chosen.' The Son is undertaking to become man; it is to be a covenant by sacrifice. He undertakes in our behalf, and for us: the promise of eternal life and the Holy Spirit are to come upon him; this the Holy Ghost undertakes to do; and these are to abide upon him, the head of influence, till salvation is finished.

And, when Christ was glorified, then the Word and Spirit were to be sent forth by the covenant head to the chosen seed. The Spirit is to apply the benefits of the cross, and proclaim liberty to the elect; 'By the blood of thy covenant I have sent thy prisoners out of the pit wherein is no water.' They are called Christ's prisoners, because they are given unto him to redeem, sanctify, and save.

In the work of creation the distinct personality and operations of the Holy Trinity plainly appear. There is God the Father creating all things by Jesus Christ, Eph. 3:9; and there is the Holy Spirit moving upon the face of the waters, Gen. 1:2; bringing the confused chaos into its present beautiful form and order. 'By the word of the Lord were the heavens made, and all the host of them by the breath of his mouth', Psalm 33:6. Here is the Lord, and the essential Word which was with God and was God, creating the world; and the breath of his mouth, which is the Holy Ghost, equally concerned in the work; for, 'By his Spirit he hath garnished the heavens', Job 26:13.

Nor need it be thought strange that the Holy Ghost is compared to breath and to the wind; seeing, as a learned man observes, that 'generation expresses the Son's distinct mode of subsisting in the divine essence, so spiration may also express the Spirit's distinct mode of subsisting therein; and, perhaps is the true reason of his bearing this name.' And, as he is called the breath of the Almighty, and as Christ breathed on the apostles and said unto them, 'Receive ye the Holy Ghost'; the procession of the Holy Spirit is beautifully set forth thereby.

There was a council held among the divine Persons about the creation of man. 'Let us', says the Father to the Son, 'make man in our image, after our likeness'; and the Holy Ghost was breathed into him, who formed his soul and quickened him.

'So God created man in his own image, in the image of God created he him.' In those words, 'Let us make man in our image, after our likeness', a plurality of Persons appears; but in the last text, 'So God made man in his own image', the unity of the divine essence is preserved; the first account being in the plural number, and the last in the singular.

In the government of the world the Trinity appears to be equally concerned. This may be seen in the king of Babylon's visions; 'I saw in the visions of my head, upon my bed; and, behold, a Watcher and an Holy One came down from heaven.' This is in the singular number. 'This matter', says Daniel, 'is by the decree of the Watchers, and the demand by the word of the Holy Ones; to the intent that the living may know that the Most High ruleth in the kingdom of men, and giveth it to whomsoever he will', Dan. 4:13,17.

I know that many are of opinion that these Watchers are angels; but that cannot be; for the decree is called the decree of the Watchers, and the demand by the words of the Holy Ones; but angels are not of God's council, nor have they any hand in making God's decrees. 'Who hath directed the Spirit of the Lord; or, being his counsellor, hath taught him? With whom took he counsel, and who instructed him?' Isa. 40:13,14. What is called the decree of the Watchers and of the Holy Ones, is explained by the prophet. 'This is the decree of the Most High, which is come upon my lord the king.'

Besides, though the angels are holy creatures, yet three of them cannot be emphatically called the Holy Ones, for there are twenty thousand of holy angels, and there are holy souls in heaven and holy saints on earth. But God in three Persons is the fountain of holiness. Nor need we wonder at the Trinity being called Watchers, seeing God the Father, Son, and Spirit, watch over all the saints. He that keepeth thee will not slumber. 'Behold, he that keepeth Israel shall neither slumber nor sleep.' And, unless the Lord keep the city of Zion, all other watchmen awake but in vain. Thus doth the Holy Trinity work jointly together, and their distinct personality is seen in all their glorious works; and so it will further appear in every branch of the work of salvation.

As in the mission and commission of Christ; 'From the time that it was, there am I: and now the Lord GOD and his Spirit hath sent me', Isa. 48:16. Here is Christ—me—that is sent, and here is the Lord God, and here also his Spirit which sent him. If a trinity of names is meant and not persons, as a wise man observes, it should have been worded thus: 'And now I myself, and myself, have sent myself.' This prophecy had its accomplishment just before Christ entered on his ministry, at his baptism. Christ was upon the earth, the Holy Ghost descending in a bodily shape like a dove upon him, and a voice came from heaven, saying, 'Thou art my beloved Son, in thee I am well pleased.' These are the Lord God and his Spirit sending Christ forth, and bearing their testimony both to his Sonship and to his appointment.

Salvation also is ascribed to all the three Persons, who are equally concerned in it. The Father speaks thus: 'But I will have mercy on the house of Judah, and will save them by the Lord their God; and will not save them by bow, nor by sword, nor by battle, nor by horses, nor by horsemen', Hosea 1:7. Thus the Father bears testimony to his only begotten Son, and tells us that he is the Lord God by whom he saves us; and we believe him, not doubting but God is a faithful and true witness, and must be a better judge of his own Son, and what he is, than all the Arians and Socinians in the world. God the Father saves us by the Lord our God, who is the Son; hence he is called Jesus, because he shall save his people from their sins, Mt. 1:21.

Nor is the Holy Ghost excluded from the work of salvation; for the Father, who tells us that he will have mercy upon the house of Judah, tells us also how his mercy shall come to us, even by the Holy Spirit; 'But according to his mercy he saved us, by the washing of regeneration and renewing of the Holy Ghost', Titus 3:5. Thus are all the three divine Persons engaged in our salvation. Hence we read of wells, more wells than one, in which salvation is to be had; 'Therefore with joy shall ye draw water out of the wells of salvation.'

Again an empty name cannot write nor bear record. How does a fictitious name appear in a court of law, when there is no person to be found that bears that name, or is called by it? 'But there are three that bear record in heaven; the Father, the Word, and the Holy Ghost; and these three are one.' And this is not a trinity of names accommodated to the making of a covenant, as some suppose; for a name cannot be a father nor a son. So, likewise, if there be but one Person in the Trinity, there cannot be either a Son or a Father; he that denies either, denies both. 'He is antichrist that denieth the Father and the Son: whosoever denieth the Son, the same hath not the Father', I John 2:22,23.

None, therefore, but persons can bear record; but the Persons in the Holy Trinity do bear record; and the record that they bear is to the Sonship of Christ; and their distinct record stands in the holy scriptures. The Father's record, twice written, is this; 'Thou art my beloved Son, in thee I am well pleased', Luke 3:22. Again, 'This is my beloved Son, in whom I am well pleased; hear ye him', Mt. 17:5. The Lord's testimony of himself stands upon record thus: 'Say ye of him, whom the

Father hath sanctified and sent into the world, Thou blasphemest; because I said, I am the Son of God? If I do not the works of my Father, believe me not', John 10:36,37. For this blasphemy, as the wicked Jews called it, was Christ condemned; and this he never denied, but sealed it with his blood.

The record of the Holy Ghost is to the same truth. 'Paul, a servant separated unto the gospel of God, which he promised afore by his prophets in the holy scriptures, concerning his Son Jesus Christ our Lord, which was made of the seed of David according to the flesh; and declared to be the Son of God with power, according to the Spirit of holiness, by the resurrection from the dead', Rom. 1:1-4. This is the witness which is recorded by the Spirit that Christ is the Son of God; not in name, for there is no power in an empty name; but he is the Son of God with power, the omnipotent, 'The first and the last, the Almighty.' And this is declared, or manifested, by his own resurrection from the dead; 'Destroy this temple, and in three days I will raise it up': this is the testimony borne and recorded by the Spirit of holiness.

Now that the threefold record, borne by the Father, Son, and Spirit, is to the Sonship of Christ, appears plain from the Apostle John's conclusion: 'There are three that bear record in heaven, and three that bear witness on earth. If we receive the witness of men, the witness of God is greater: for this is the witness of God which he hath testified of his Son. He that believeth on the Son of God hath the witness in himself; he that believeth not God hath made himself a liar, because he believeth not the record that God gave of his Son', I John 5:7-10. Thus God's witness, that he hath testified, and which stands upon record, is called the testimony and record that God gave of his Son.

The natural inferences are these:

1. That none but those who believe in the only begotten Son of God have the witness of the Spirit in themselves.

2. That all those who tell us that Christ is only a name, or a mere creature, are infidels; they believe not the record that God gave of his Son. And,

3. The infamy charged upon such is, that they make God a liar, than which nothing can be worse; and such liars are all Arians and Socinians, and therefore their witness is nothing worth.

Thus the holy Three bear record, which a trinity of names cannot do; for, as I before observed, if a fictitious name appear in a court of law they can do nothing with it, being but an empty name: and it must be some person or other that must have written that; but the Holy Trinity want none to write for them, unless it be in condescension to our weakness, for they can all write for themselves. Thus saith God the Father: 'But this shall be the covenant that I will make with the house of Israel; After those days, saith the LORD, I will put my law in their inward parts, and write it in their hearts; and will be their God, and they shall be my people', Jer. 31:33.

And God the Son promises to write the following inscription upon all conquerors: 'Him that overcometh will I make a pillar in the temple of my God, and he shall go no more out: and I will write upon him the name of my God, and the name of the city of my God, which is new Jerusalem, which cometh down out of heaven from my God: and I will write upon him my new name', Rev. 3:12.

And the Holy Ghost's handwriting is recorded thus; 'Forasmuch as ye are manifestly declared to be the epistle of Christ ministered by us, written not with ink, but with the Spirit of the living God; not in tables of stone, but in fleshy tables of the heart', II Cor. 3:3. The law that God puts into the hidden parts is shedding abroad his everlasting love in our hearts (love being the fulfilling of the law) by the Holy Ghost given unto us. Writing his law in the mind, is persuading us by his Spirit, and working in us the law of faith: 'The Lord shall persuade Japheth, and he shall dwell in the tents of Shem.' What Habakkuk was ordered to write plain upon tables, that he who runs might read, God writes on the fleshy tables of our hearts, by justifying us and giving us faith and life; and in this the vision speaks in our conscience, 'The just shall live by his faith.'

Christ writes upon us the name of his God; that is, he gives us an experience of that glorious covenant-name which God proclaimed before Moses, 'The Lord, the Lord God, gracious and merciful, slow to anger, abundant in goodness and truth; pardoning iniquity, transgression and sin.' Pardon comes by the blood of Christ; grace, goodness, and mercy, all come together when God reveals his dear Son in us.

To write upon us the name of the city of God, is to give us the happy enjoyment of peace, which is the fruit and effect of imputed righteousness; and to bless us with the presence of God. The city is to be called Jehovah Shammah, the Lord is there; or the city of God's presence; God promising to dwell in Zion for ever, it being his resting place, and he having desired it.

The Lord's new name seems to be that worn upon his vesture and on his thigh, and is, 'King of kings, and Lord of lords'; which name he will achieve by the destruction of antichrist, and taking to himself his great power and reigning, when the kingdoms of this world will become his; and he then will make his children princes in all the earth.

This greatest of all kingdoms, bigger than the Babylonian, Grecian, or Roman, will be given to the saints of the Most High, who shall take it and possess it for ever and ever; then the saints will be kings, and rule over their oppressors.

Making them pillars, is polishing them by grace, making them upright and ornamental in their profession; and where these things are found written by the Holy Spirit on the fleshy tables of the heart, the sum and substance of the New Testament, whether in the gospels or in the epistles of the apostles, are experienced in the souls of God's elect, which makes them the pillar and ground of the truth known and read of all men, being made manifest in the consciences both of saints and sinners, hypocrites and heretics.

And such living epistles have a seal upon them, as all epistles should have, having the broad seal of heaven on their souls, by which they become God's secret treasure, being sealed up to the day of redemption, which is redemption from the grave.

These things are recorded by the Holy Trinity, and these things are written in the minds and hearts of all believers; and these inscriptions are as puzzling to the wise and prudent among us, as the handwriting upon the walls of Belshazzar's palace was to the wise men of Babylon. But messengers who bear such tidings, and interpreters to explain them, are scarce. 'If there be a messenger with him, an interpreter, one among a thousand, to show unto man his uprightness, then he is gracious unto him.'

And I think that, if every congregated thousand in a profession in this nation had a real messenger to bring forth such good tidings, and endowed with divine skill to interpret them to sinners in whose hearts they are written, old England would be one of the happiest countries in all the world.

the fifth meditation

V

The Fifth Meditation

I SHOWED in my last meditation how all Persons in the glorious Trinity were jointly concerned in the salvation of God's elect; and treated a little of their co-operation in every branch of it. And this will further appear, even in the application of the promises. 'The words of the wise are as goads, and as nails fastened by the masters of assemblies, which are given from one shepherd', Eccl. 12:11. In the masters of assemblies a plurality of persons appear; but in the one shepherd the unity of God is seen.

If it be replied, that by the masters of assemblies the Jewish doctors are meant; I answer, they were not preachers of God's word; they made that of none effect by their own traditions. Nor can it mean the apostles or ordinary gospel ministers, for they dare not take the title of master: 'Be not ye called Rabbi, for one is your master, even Christ.'

Nor is it in the power of any man to apply the word of God. To fasten the word of God, as a nail driven up to the head, requires power; and the excellency of the power is of God, and not of us. If the most eloquent orator in the world, by the dint of elocution, was to attempt this work, and move the passions of men to the uttermost, all that can be said of it is, that they received it in word only. But when the word comes with power, in the Holy Ghost, and in much assurance, the nail is fastened; nor is it possible for either men or devils to draw it out.

God the Father calls himself a master. 'If I be a master, where is my fear?' Mal. 1:6. Call no man master, for one is your master, even Christ, Mt. 23:10. And so he that is taught of the Spirit sows to the Spirit, and is led by the Spirit; he learns, obeys, and follows his master.

Now these words of the wise, called goads, that prick; and nails, that hold fast, are given from one shepherd, even God: The Lord is my shepherd, therefore I shall not want; for we are the people of his pasture, and the sheep of his hand.

Again. We are baptized in the Name of all the Three divine Persons. 'Go ye therefore, and teach all nations, baptizing them in the name of the Father, and of the Son, and of the Holy Ghost', Mt. 28:19. And, when we are baptized with the Holy Ghost and with fire, the love of God is shed abroad in the heart; the sun of righteousness arises with healing in his beams, and shines like the sun in his full strength; when the Holy Ghost brings the live coal from off the altar, or puts both life and love in the word, and lays it upon our tongue, telling us that our iniquity is taken away, and our sin purged, and that we must now confess it, and proclaim it. This baptism makes a minister a flaming fire, a burning and shining light; and unites poor souls to Father, Son, and Holy Ghost; and interests them in the love of all Three.

But besides the baptism of the Holy Ghost, there is another that follows, and that is the fiery trial. We read of the spirit of judgment, and of the spirit of burning: for God keeps his fire in Zion and his furnace in Jerusalem, that his real churches may not be overrun with tares and chaff, straw and stubble.

The vessels of gold and of silver will stand the furnace, but the vessels of wood and of earth will consume: the former, by losing their dross, appear the brighter and better for the fire; the latter, like a fool brayed in a morter, ten times worse.

This blessed mystery ever was, and ever will be with the chosen of God; for thus it is written: 'According to the word that I covenanted with you when ye came out of Egypt, so my Spirit remaineth among you: fear ye not. For thus saith the Lord of Hosts; It is a little while, and I will shake the heavens, and the earth, the sea, and the dry land. And I will shake all nations, and the desire of all nations shall come', Haggai 2:5-7.

Here is God the Father speaking and covenanting; and the essential Word, who is the covenant head and the covenant itself; because the covenant is with him, made with him, confirmed by him, and all the blessings of it are in him. The glorious proclamation of the name of the Lord is nothing else but the mercy and blessings of God in Christ Jesus, held forth in the covenant of grace: and this my name, says God, is in him; in the angel that went before them.

Hence they are charged to obey him, and not to provoke him, for he will not pardon your transgressions. When Moses calls Christ the Rock, whose work is perfect; and sets him before them as their refuge, their life, and the length of their days; and tells them not to say in their heart, 'Who shall ascend into heaven, or who shall descend into the deep?' to fetch the Word to them; these are all applied in the New Testament to Christ, and are the things of the new covenant, which the Spirit applies to the elect of God. Here is the Lord of Hosts speaking, and the Word, Christ, spoken of, and called the desire of all nations; and the covenant with him; and the Spirit remaining still among them: for although national mercies were often taken away from Israel, and national calamities brought on, yet the elect were never deserted of their God.

Moreover, the Holy Trinity are to be considered in all our addresses or approaches to God: 'For through him we both have access by one Spirit unto the Father.' Here is the Father, to whom we find nearness and access, the Surety having removed our sins and a broken law out of the way, and appearing as our peacemaker and mediator, through whom we are indulged with this access; and here is one Spirit, under whose influence, as a spirit of grace and supplication, we draw nigh.

This is the new and living way which Christ hath consecrated: and he tells us that no man can come to the Father but by him; and he that enters not by this new way and strait gate, but climbs up some other way, the same is a thief and a robber; and such thieves and robbers are the Arians, Socinians, and Papists; the former allowing of no mediator, and the latter bringing in a hundred.

This mystery, my dearly beloved, we must keep, hold fast, and abide in; which is so clearly revealed in the word of God. For, 'If that which ye have heard from the beginning shall remain in you, ye shall also continue in the Son and in the Father; but the anointing teacheth you of all things, and is truth, and is no lie: and even as it hath taught you, ye shall abide in him.'

Hence we may conclude, that whosoever hath not the doctrine of Christ hath not God; but he that hath the doctrine of Christ, who receives the love of the truth, or the love of God, which is promised to us in the word of truth; and he that receives the truth in the love of it, believes in it, and holds it fast, confesseth it, and abides in it, even he shall continue in the Son, and in the Father; and likewise he shall continue in the anointing, which is truth, and is no lie.

But I must break off, and go to our gates, where there are things new and old, which are laid up for the king's beloved, that a portion of meat in due season may be given to the household.

the sixth meditation

VI

The Sixth Meditation

I CONCLUDED my last meditation with our abiding in the Son and in the Father, and, likewise, in the anointing, which is truth, and is no lie. Now I shall proceed, beginning with the apostolic benediction: 'The grace of our Lord Jesus Christ, and the love of God, and the communion of the Holy Ghost, be with you all', which is of the same import. Now from all these plain passages of scripture, which I have quoted, three divine persons appear in one God, and no more; none can be left out, nor can one be added.

But the adversaries to the Trinity object, because the express word Trinity is not mentioned in the bible. However it is not the word that they hate and fight against, but the doctrine. We know that two is a couple, or a pair; three is a trinity; and four a quaternity: and, 'There are three that bear record in heaven', and no more, 'and these three are one'; not three names and one person, but three distinct persons in one undivided essence.

So likewise they object to the word Satisfaction, that is, satisfaction by the sacrifice of Christ; because the express word is not mentioned. But the thing is to be found in the bible. God is called a creditor, Luke 7:41; and poor sinners are debtors; that is, to fulfil the whole law. 'He that offends in one point is guilty of all.' Should sinners die in this state, into the prison of hell they must go. For, if we die in our sins, then where Christ is we cannot come; and therefore cannot come out of prison, no, not till the very last mite is paid. As lying in jail, we cannot pay debts: hence, there can be no hope of a jail delivery. All men are exposed to this, and threatened with it, while in their sins.

In this state Christ found us when he took our nature, and was made of a woman, and made under the law. Our sins he took, and bore them in his own body on the tree, and was made a curse for us, and died in our room, the just for the unjust, and so redeemed us from the curse, fulfilling all righteousness, with which our creditor is well pleased. By the blood of his covenant he sends forth his elect prisoners out of the pit, declaring himself faithful and just in forgiving sins, and in cleansing from all unrighteousness. And this is real satisfaction made for sin, for the creditor is well pleased with it; and to be well pleased with the payment is to be satisfied with it.

And, as these things are found, we hold the words which well express them; and it pleases God, by the foolishness of preaching these things, to save all those who believe in them. And, on the other hand, we find many things advanced by those who are opposite to us, which sound as bad in our ears as the words Person, Trinity, and Satisfaction, do in theirs.

Some tell us that Christ was only an instrument in the creation, or a creating instrument. Nothing can sound worse in the ears of a true lover of Christ than this. It is not common sense. We know that instruments are used by mechanics and builders, to fit and prepare materials for the purpose the artist or builder intends them: but to tell a man that such a mechanic has finished such a curious machine, and that such a building is erected, to be the property of the tools that were used in the work, and for the praise and glory of them, would appear madness.

So to talk of a creating instrument, or an instrument possessing creating power to make all things out of nothing, are such things as no man in his senses can believe. 'For by him were all things created that are in heaven, and that are in earth, visible and invisible, whether they be thrones, or dominions, or principalities, or powers: all things were created by him, and for him: and he is before all things, and by him all things consist', Col. 1:16,17. He is here declared to be before all things; and of course long before this creating instrument could be invented, or brought forth. 'All things were created by him, and for him'; created by his own power, and for his own glory and use: 'and by him all things consist', or are preserved in their existence.

Now this glorious Creator cannot be an instrument, but he must be God: and to this the Father bears witness. 'But unto the Son he saith, Thy throne, O God, is for ever and ever; a sceptre of righteousness is the sceptre of thy kingdom; thou hast loved righteousness, and hated iniquity; therefore God, even thy God, hath anointed thee with the oil of gladness above thy fellows. And, thou, Lord, in the beginning hast laid the foundation of the earth; and the heavens are the works of thy hands. They shall perish, but thou remainest; and they shall all wax old as doth a garment; and as a vesture shalt thou fold them up, and they shall be changed: but thou art the same, and thy years shall not fail', Heb. 1:8-12.

In the above words God the Father calls the divine Creator of heaven and earth, God and Lord; and tells us, that the heavens are the work of his hands: and he must be the best judge of his own Son. They tell us that Christ had a human soul pre-existing from eternity, and that it was with this that God took counsel, and by this he made the world. But Christ is before all things, which this thing cannot be; much less can it be called the fellow of the LORD of hosts. And surely it must be robbery with a witness, for such a thing as this to make itself equal with God, as Christ did, even when he made himself of no reputation, and took on him the form of a servant, Phil. 2:7.

Some talk of Christ's being a delegated power, and a subordinate God, and a God by office; but this is making more gods than one: for, if one be supreme and the other subordinate, there must be two; different in essence, glory, power, and majesty. And to worship with divine adoration any thing below infinite divinity, is rank idolatry. However, this vain-imagined distinction between the Father and Son hath no place in the bible. The LORD of hosts calls Christ his fellow, Zech. 13:7. And Christ thought it not robbery to be equal with God the Father, Phil. 2:6. Christ says, 'I and my Father are one.'

And, all men must honour the Son, even as they honour the Father. And if he is truly and properly God, equal to the Father, and one with him, and always in him, then there can be no idolatry in worshipping him; for all the angels of God are commanded to worship the firstborn, even in his state of incarnation; as they all did at his birth, Heb. 1:6.

And Zion is commanded to do the same; and the true reason given for this command is, because he is God: 'He is thy Jehovah, and worship thou him', Psalm 45:11. And we know that, 'The LORD our God is one LORD', Deut. 6:4. And we must have no other gods but him: 'Thou shalt worship the LORD thy God, and him only shalt thou serve.' And he that obeys this first and great commandment must banish far from his mind all the spurious deities of the Arians and Socinians, for these are no better than the image which Nebuchadnezzar the king had set up.

Many such strange notions as these does Satan beget in the vain imaginations of men; and such are inventors of evil things, and set up the stumblingblock of their iniquity in their heart; and God takes them in their own craftiness, by suffering them to pay adoration to that which is not God; which is idolatry, and an image of jealousy: which the pure gospel, if ever it had been attended with power to their hearts, would have pulled down. 'For the weapons of our warfare are mighty through God to the pulling down of strong holds; casting down imaginations, and every high thing that exalteth itself against the knowledge of God, and bringing into captivity every thought to the obedience of Christ.'

And sure I am that those who deny the eternity of Christ, and talk of a human soul pre-existing, talk nonsense. No human soul can be God's fellow, nor God's equal, nor one with him, nor one in him. Much less can such a creature, which is inferior to an angel, be the only begotten Son of God, or the Son of the Father in truth and love. But, as for Christ, 'All things were made by him, and he is before all things.' We are not to hope in a creature, but to set our hope in God.

Christ is the faithful and true witness, and the record that he bears of himself is true; and this is the record that he bears of himself: 'I am Alpha and Omega, the beginning and the ending, saith the Lord, which is, and which was, and which is to come: the Almighty', Rev. 1:8.

The enemies to the glorious mystery of the Trinity hold a trinity, only they allow of three names, yet but one Person. Nor are they agreed which is the Person: some Sabellians hold Christ to be the Person, and the Father and the Spirit to be only names. Some, that are called Arians and Socinians, say the Father is the Person, and the Son and Spirit are but names:

thus one denies the Father, and the other denies the Son; and between these two they have no God.

This, however, must be true, that whatsoever the Father is, the Son must be the same; and so the Jews understood the Saviour's confession of his own sonship, and laid this thing to his charge, namely, that he made himself equal with God. 'Therefore the Jews sought the more to kill him, because he not only had broken the sabbath, but said also that God was his Father, making himself equal with God': which the Saviour denied not, but confirmed. 'The Son can do nothing of himself' —how can this be, when the Father and he are one?—'but what he seeth the Father do: for what things soever he doeth, these also doeth the Son likewise', John 5:18,19.

Hence it is plain, that the Son is equal with the Father; and, if so, then he must be of the same nature with him. So that, if the Son be a son only in name, the Father must be the same; if Christ be only a son in office, or in a figurative sense, the Father must be so too; and, if Christ be no more than a human soul, which is but a mere creature, the Father must be such also. For Christ is declared to be the only begotten Son of God. Begotten, and not created. Nor is he a son by office, as magistrates are; nor by creation, as angels and men are; but, 'The Son of the Father in truth and love.'

Therefore, whatever the Son is, such is the Father, for Christ is the Son of the Father in truth and love: and, as the Father is God, such is Christ; 'The brightness of his glory, and the express image of his person', Heb. 1:3. 'The true God, and eternal life', I John 5:20. 'And without controversy great is the mystery of godliness: God was manifest in the flesh, justified in the Spirit, seen of angels, preached unto the Gentiles, believed on in the world, and received up into glory', I Tim. 3:16.

And, were all the Arians and Socinians in the world to combine together, they never could apply the above, nor the following ascriptions, to a human soul, or to any mere creature, however exalted or dignified. 'Keep this commandment without spot, unrebukable, until the appearing of our Lord Jesus Christ: which in his times he shall show, who is the blessed and only Potentate, the King of kings, and Lord of lords; who only hath immortality, dwelling in the light which no man can approach unto; whom no man hath seen, nor can see; to whom be honour and power everlasting. Amen', I Tim. 6:14-16.

Let all the enemies of the Son of God prove that an empty name, or a pre-existing human soul, or a demi-god, or a god by office, or a creating instrument, or a subordinate god: let them, I say, choose out of this list of imaginary deities which they please, and let them prove that the apostle's ascriptions are applicable to their feigned gods, namely, that their pre-existing human soul is the blessed and only Potentate; that this creature is the King of kings, and Lord of lords; that this human soul hath only immortality; that it dwells in the light which no man can approach unto, whom no man hath seen nor can see; and that honour and power everlasting, Amen, is to be ascribed to that; 'He feedeth on ashes: a deceived heart hath turned him aside, that he cannot deliver his soul, nor say, Is there not a lie in my right hand?' Isaiah 44:20.

Nor did the incarnation of Christ bring a fourth person into the Trinity. The human nature of Christ is not a person; it is called a new thing, Jer. 31:22, and a holy thing, Luke 1:35, but not a person; for the human nature of Christ never had personal subsistence, or it never did personally exist alone or of itself, but it subsisted in union with the divine Person of the Son of God: 'The Word was made flesh.'

Some tell us that Christ took on him a human form from everlasting; but how he could assume a human form, when there were no human beings, is what I cannot conceive; there can be no form of a thing that never existed, any more than the sun could have a shadow from everlasting when the sun had no being.

I read that Christ was found in the form of God, and that he thought it not robbery to be equal with God. And this form does not mean any outward shape; for, 'Who hath heard God's voice, or seen his shape?' But it means that he possessed, in the highest degree, all divine perfections which are peculiar to the divine being; 'Being the brightness of his (the Father's) glory, and the express image of his person.'

What has led some poor, blind, presumptuous souls into this mistake is, the Saviour's being seen by Abraham and by Joshua in a human appearance: and by the same rule they might prove that he assumed the nature and form of angels from everlasting; for he appeared to Moses, to Jacob, and to Manoah, as an angel of God. But the truth is, the Son then was neither angel nor man; not an angel, because he is the creator of angels: 'He maketh his angels spirits, and his ministers a flaming fire'; nor a man, for as such he never had personal subsistence or existence.

But they tell us that the human soul of Christ, and the form of a human body which Christ took from everlasting, and which they call 'the glory man', and in which he appeared to the ancient patriarchs, was part of our nature; so that, when he became incarnate, he took only a human body not a reasonable soul; which they prove from these words; 'For verily he took not on him the nature of angels.' 'Human souls', they say, 'are angelic; but he took not on him the nature of angels.'

But, if this can be any proof, we shall not know what the scriptures mean by things; there is a distinction between an innumerable company of angels, and the spirits of just men made perfect. Nor are the souls of men ever called angels, though ministers of the gospel are; but even this respects their office, not their nature; for both angels and preachers are ministers to the heirs of salvation; but preachers are only angels by office, not by nature.

Nor can it be proved from the words of Christ, when he says, 'They neither marry, nor are given in marriage; but are as the angels of God in heaven'; for this only respects their glorified state: and the words were intended to confound the Sadducees, who asked, Whose wife of the seven the woman should be in the resurrection?

The Saviour informs them that marriage is peculiar to this life, and for the procreation of children; but in the world to come there would be no more of this than there is among the angels. Otherwise there will be a great deal of difference between angels and saints; the former being the Lord's servants, the latter the Lord's wife: 'Thy Maker is thine husband; the LORD of hosts is his name'; but this never was said of angels.

One would wonder, were it not for the power and dominion that the devil has over mankind, how any man dare to assert such things in plain contradiction to the word of God. For, if this human bodily form and the human soul of Christ were from eternity, and nothing taken at his incarnation but the body, how can this scripture be true; 'Wherefore, in all things it behoved him to be made like unto his brethren', when there was none of his brethren ever made like unto him? And, if this behoved him, if it was meet and fit it should be so, it ill becomes men to make such a difference.

Nor could Adam be a figure of him that was to come; for Adam came not into being this way. Adam, Christ's figure, was made body and soul at once, and all Christ's brethren come into the world with a body and a soul; and they are all born under the law and under the curse of it, being by this natural birth children of wrath even as others; and the heaviest sentence of the law is levelled at the soul, 'The soul that sins shall die.'

Now Christ, as our surety, must be made like unto his brethren; and so he was; he was made of a woman, and made under the law, to redeem them that were under the law, by making his soul an offering for sin; and then he was to see of the travail of his soul and be satisfied.

But, if his human soul existed from eternity, it was not made under the law, and therefore could not be subjected, by virtue of his suretyship engagements, to endure the wrath and curse of God for us. They that suffer the law, whether they suffer as surety or as debtors, must be made under the law, and be subject to the law. Men have bodies and souls, and both are under the law, and both have sinned. And he that redeems them must be of the same nature with them, and near of kin to them, or the former institution of God will not admit of it. He that redeems must be a brother, or one near of kin, Lev. 25:48,49. Christ is both brother and kinsman; but a human body is neither a brother nor a kinsman, it is only half brother, and the worst half; yea, a dead brother, for, 'The body without the spirit is dead', James 2:26.

The truth is, Christ took not on him the nature of angels to redeem fallen angels, but he took on him the seed of Abraham, the whole human nature, body and soul; and this is plain by the growth of both: for, 'Jesus increased in wisdom and stature, and in favour with God and man', Luke 2:52. His soul grew in wisdom and his body grew in stature; but, if his soul had existed from all eternity, his wisdom and understanding must have been mature and fully ripe before the world began, and therefore incapable of such a growth.

the seventh meditation

VII

The Seventh Meditation

THE damnable heresy of denying the divinity of our Lord and Saviour seems to me to render him of no use in any one of his office characters; it renders, also, his great undertaking and his finished work neither meritorious nor efficacious; for no mere creature can merit for himself, much less for another. His divine nature stamps infinite dignity on all his office characters, and so it does on all his mighty works.

His kingly office stands on this; 'But unto the Son he saith, thy throne, O God, is for ever and ever; a sceptre of righteousness is the sceptre of thy kingdom.' Which kingdom stands in power, and is always called the kingdom of God. 'His name shall be called Wonderful, Counsellor, The mighty God, The everlasting Father, the Prince of Peace; of the increase of his government and peace there shall be no end, upon the throne of David, and upon his kingdom, to order it, and to establish it with judgment and with justice, from henceforth even for ever. The zeal of the LORD of hosts will perform this', Isa. 9:6,7. Hence he is called King of Zion, and King of glory.

The merit and dignity of his priestly office proceeds on the same footing. How could any mere man's dying atone for all the transgressions that were committed under the first testament, and all the sins of God's elect under the second? Insomuch as those that are called do receive the promise of eternal inheritance,

Heb. 9:15. Hence it is asserted that by his one offering he hath perfected for ever all them that are sanctified. The dignity of his office and the merits of his oblation spring from his divine sonship. 'For the law maketh men high priests which have infirmities; but the word of the oath, which was since the law, maketh the Son, who is consecrated for evermore', Heb. 7:28.

His prophetic office, and the perfection of it, proceeds on the foundation of his proper deity. 'The LORD came from Sinai, and rose up from Seir unto them; he shined forth from mount Paran, and he came with ten thousands of saints; from his right hand went a fiery law for them. Yea, he loved the people; all his saints are in thy hand: and they sat down at thy feet; every one shall receive of thy words', Deut. 33:2,3.

At this divine prophet's feet did Mary sit, and receive of his word, when Martha was cumbered with much serving. And in allusion to this text is Mary commended, and is said to choose the good part, which shall not be taken from her. She was a disciple that was brought up at the Lord's feet; and, as all God's children are taught of the Lord, Mary was one of his family, who could never be deprived either of the word of life which she received, nor yet of her adoption into God's family; she was an heir of promise, and a child of God.

And who but the only begotten Son could reveal and make known God's counsel and covenant, his good will of purpose and of promise; his tender mercy, lovingkindness, pity, and compassion, which were but dimly known under the former dispensation? And that God is love, I John 4:8, was not known, at least not recorded, under the first testament. 'All things are delivered unto me of my Father; and no man knoweth the Son but the Father; neither knoweth any man the Father save the Son, and he to whomsoever the Son will reveal him', Matt. 11:27.

His office of mediator could stand us in no stead if he were not Immanuel, God with us. The breach opened by sin between God and man was infinite, as the scriptures witness. 'Is not thy wickedness great? and thine iniquity infinite?' Our sin had separated between us and our God. Moses, indeed, was at times allowed to stand in the gap; but it was by virtue of his office, in which he personated the Saviour, that he was suffered to mediate there; and, though at times he prevailed to lengthen out Israel's tranquillity, yet judgment always overtook them at last. 'I have pardoned according to thy word.' But they have tempted me now these ten times, surely they shall not see the land, Numbers 14:20, 22, 23.

No prayer of Moses, Noah, Daniel, or Job, will purge our sins, magnify the law, or satisfy divine justice. He that stands in this breach, and lays his hand upon both, must be God's equal, Phil. 2:6, and man's fellow, Psalm 45:7; or else mercy and truth will never meet together, nor will righteousness and peace kiss each other. But Christ was the mighty God when a child born, and the prince of life when crucified, Acts 3:15; the Holy One, who saw no corruption, when in the tomb, Psalm 16:10. It was truth that sprung out of the earth at his resurrection, when righteousness looked down from heaven well pleased, Psalm 85:11. He was God manifest in the flesh when he was received up into glory, I Tim. 3:16. And the Lord of hosts and King of glory when he entered there, Psalm 24:9,10. And we can have no better proof of all this than by seeing poor prisoners come forth out of the pit in which is no water, by the blood of his covenant, Zech. 9:11.

And sure I am that his being our advocate with the Father, if he be no more than a creature, would never be sufficient to silence law and justice, Satan and conscience: but as he is the wonderful Counsellor, and the mighty God, he can do it, and, blessed be his precious name, we know that he has done it, and will do it.

His endearing character of a husband is founded on the same divine basis; 'Thy Maker is thine husband; the LORD of hosts is his name, the God of the whole earth shall he be called.'

His character of a father stands on the same bottom; 'The second Adam, the quickening Spirit, the Lord from heaven'; hence called the mighty God, and everlasting Father, the Prince of peace.

And that of a Saviour must needs stand on the same footing; 'God has laid help upon one that is mighty.' For how can a creature save? 'Vain is the help of man', Psalm 108:12. 'In that day it shall be said to Jerusalem, Fear thou not; and to Zion, Let not thine hands be slack. The LORD thy God, in the midst of thee is mighty; he will save, he will rejoice over thee with joy; he will rest in his love, he will joy over thee with singing', Zeph. 3:16,17.

The efficacy of his blood springs from the same divine source; for, though he was put to death only in the flesh, yet his human nature suffered in union with his divine person. 'Take heed, therefore, unto yourselves, and to all the flock over the which the Holy Ghost hath made you overseers, to feed the church of God, which he hath purchased with his own blood', Acts 20:28.

The efficacy and excellency of everlasting righteousness takes its divinity and dignity from hence: 'Who, being in the form of God, thought it not robbery to be equal with God: but made himself of no reputation, and took upon him the form of a servant, and was made in the likeness of men: and being found in fashion as a man, he humbled himself, and became obedient unto death, even the death of the cross', Phil. 2:6-8. From hence springs the glory and efficacy of his obedience; yea, 'In the Lord shall all the seed of Israel be justified and shall glory'; for he has brought in an everlasting righteousness, which takes its name from the divine nature. 'I am not ashamed of the gospel of Christ, for therein is the righteousness of God revealed from faith to faith.'

As head over all things to the church, what comfort could flow to it from the consideration of Christ being a mere man? She is exposed to thousands of inveterate adversaries, ghostly and bodily; and continually floating upon the waves and billows of trouble and distress, and deemed as the filth and offscouring of all things, and treated accordingly: while Christ, the head, is ascended far above all heavens, and of course at an infinite distance from his well beloved, if he be no more than man. No comfort can flow to her but from his immensity and omnipresence; 'Behold I am with you always to the world's end'; which, as man, abstractedly considered, he cannot be.

As a physician, who is God's way upon earth, and his saving health among all nations, Psalm 67:2. Who bore our sins and took our infirmities, and who binds up the broken-hearted and restores health to us; which cannot be done but by purging us from all our guilt and filth, idols and dead works, false notions of God and a dead form of godliness; the comfort of all which springs from his being God. 'If thou wilt diligently hearken to the voice of the LORD thy God, and wilt do that which is right in his sight, and wilt give ear to his commandments and keep all his statutes; I will put none of these diseases upon thee, which I have brought upon the Egyptians: for I am the LORD that healeth thee', Exodus 15:26.

As the covenant head: 'Thou spakest in vision to thy holy one, and saidst, I have laid help upon one that is mighty; I have exalted one chosen out of the people. Also, I will make him my firstborn higher than the kings of the earth. My mercy will I keep for him for evermore, and my covenant shall stand fast with him. His seed will I also make to endure for ever, and his throne as the days of heaven', Psalm 89. Which covenant is a covenant of royalty; the Lord is king, and the elect are subjects. A covenant of wedlock, in which the Lord of hosts is the husband and the elect the wife; and he betroths them unto him for ever: 'Yea I will betroth thee unto me in righteousness, and in judgment, and in lovingkindness, and in mercies. I will even betroth thee unto me in faithfulness; and thou shalt know the LORD', Hosea 2:19,20.

It is a covenant of an everlasting priesthood, in which the Son of God is high priest, and God the Holy Ghost is his anointing and consecration; and he is ordained by God the Father to this office for his elect, to make an atonement for them, to perfect them, and to intercede for them, till they are all brought, in a state of holiness and happiness, into the holy of holies, eternal in the heavens, where our high priest is for us entered. The comfort of all which springs from his being, not as Moses, who was a faithful servant; but from Christ being a son over his own house, whose house are we; and the Son over this his own house is God. 'For every house is builded by some man; but he that built all things is God', Heb. 3:4.

As an object of trust and confidence: no consolation can arise to us from his being no more than a creature; so far from it, that it is dangerous to the last degree to trust in him as such. 'For thus saith the LORD, Cursed be the man that trusteth in man, and maketh flesh his arm, and whose heart departeth from the LORD: for he shall be like the heath in the desert, and shall not see when good cometh; but shall inhabit the parched places in the wilderness, in a salt land not inhabited', Jer. 17:5,6. This is the woeful case and state of all those who deny the godhead of Christ, and yet trust in him as no more than man.

But there is no curse upon them that trust in the only begotten Son of God. 'I have set my king upon my holy hill of Zion. I will declare the decree: the LORD hath said unto me, Thou art my son; this day have I begotten thee. Be wise now therefore, O ye kings: be instructed, ye judges of the earth. Serve the LORD with fear, and rejoice with trembling. Kiss the son, lest he be angry, and ye perish from the way, when his wrath is kindled but a little. Blessed are all they that put their trust in him', Psalm 2.

Here is no curse to them that trust in the Son of God and King of Zion, but an eternal blessing; and no blessing can be upon those that trust in Christ if he be not God; but he is truly and properly God, and therefore those that trust in him are doubly blessed. 'Blessed is the man that trusteth in the LORD, and whose hope the LORD is. For he shall be as a tree planted by the waters, and that spreadeth out her roots by the river, and shall not see when heat cometh, but her leaf shall be green; and shall not be careful in the year of drought, neither shall cease from yielding fruit', Jer. 17:7,8.

As the object of the saints love. 'He that loveth father or mother, wife or children, more than me; is not worthy of me.' And adds, 'If any man come unto me, and hateth not his father and mother, and even his own life also, he cannot be my disciple.' Surely, if Christ be not God, he hath zealously affected us, but not well, for we are commanded to love the Lord our God with all our heart, and with all our soul, mind, and strength.

And, as Christ demands this love of all the saints, he must be God; and so he is; and therefore we can never love him enough. And those who dearly love the Son of God, God the Father is well pleased with: 'He that loveth me shall be loved of my Father, and I will love him, and will manifest myself to him', John 14:21. And he adds, 'The Father himself loveth you, because ye have loved me, and have believed that I came out from God', John 16:27.

As an object of prayer. Almost every recipient of bodily cure and of special grace, in the days of his flesh, prayed to him before they obtained either; and prayer is a branch of divine worship: yea they worshipped him with divine adoration, as the tenth leper that was healed, who returned to give glory to God; the woman with her bloody issue also, and the Syrophenician woman; yea and all the apostles, also, on the mount of Olivet, when he was taken from them up into heaven, worshipped him as he went up.

And all the heavenly host worshipped the firstborn when he was brought into the world; and Stephen, that evangelical deacon, breathed out the following petition to him, with his expiring breath, saying, Lord Jesus, receive my spirit. And he kneeled down, and cried with a loud voice, Lord, lay not this sin to their charge. And when he had said this he fell asleep. But we need not wonder at Stephen putting up his last prayer to Christ; Stephen knew him, and had the spirit of supplication in him; and the Spirit always testifies of Christ, and glorifies him also, 'He shall glorify me.'

And besides, Stephen had a view of the Saviour; he saw the heavens open, and Jesus standing at the right hand of God. And we know that, if Christ be not God, he could not be admitted to the right hand of the majesty on high, Heb. 1:3.

Hence it is plain, that all who debase the Saviour to the level of a mere creature are ignorant of him; they have never known him nor seen him. But all believers do see him, though not in that miraculous manner Stephen did. 'Yet a little while and the world seeth me no more; but ye see me: and because I live ye shall live also', John 14:19.

As a foundation. What security could a perishing sinner expect by venturing his eternal all upon any thing less than God? A human arm, and all human works, are but a sandy foundation, which must give way when the fiery trial, the dying hour and the day of judgment come to try it. But Christ is an elect, precious, tried stone, and a sure foundation; but not as a mere man; 'For who is God, save the LORD? And who is a rock, save our God', II Sam. 22:32.

He that ventures here is safe, for the gates of hell shall never prevail, either against the foundation or the superstructure. 'Whosoever heareth these sayings of mine, and doeth them, is like unto a wise man, which built his house upon a rock; and when the rains descended, and the floods came, and the winds blew and beat upon that house, it fell not, for it was founded upon a rock', Mt. 7:24,25.

In all this, my dearly beloved, I have endeavoured, as far as God hath enabled me, to cast up the highway, in opposition to them who obscure and destroy the way of our paths. But we have the promise that some shall be raised up and be enlightened, and shall be called healers of the breach, and restorers of paths to dwell in; and these are the good old paths which the just are to inquire after, and to walk in, and in which they are to find rest for their souls, Jer. 6:16.

For never surely was there more opposition made to the divinity of the Son of God, and to the power of the Holy

Ghost, than in the present day. 'But, if the foundations be destroyed, what shall the righteous do?' The wicked can rejoice in Zion's calamity; 'Rase it, Rase it, even to the foundation thereof.' But what shall the righteous do? Christ is the Lord our righteousness; and, 'He is the rock, his work is perfect; for all his ways are judgment; a God of truth, and without iniquity, just and right is he', Deut. 32:4. To remove these foundations is to strip Zion both of her ornaments and bulwarks, and to leave her as a cottage in a vineyard, or as a lodge in a garden of cucumbers, as a besieged city, Isa. 1:8.

A most daring, bold, presumptuous man, not long since, had the effrontery to declare in public, that Christ was no more God than he was; 'So far', said he, 'from his being God, he did not know the time of Jerusalem's destruction.' Alluding to the following passage, which he thought was a full proof of it: 'But of that day and that hour knoweth no man, no not the angels which are in heaven, neither the Son, but the Father', Mark 13:32.

We know that the human nature of Christ is not omniscient: as a man he grew in wisdom and in stature. I wonder this poor child of Satan did not go a little further, and prove him to be blind also; the scriptures would have borne him out according to the light which is in him, for his light is darkness. 'Who is blind, but my servant? or deaf as my messenger that I sent? Who is blind as he that is perfect, and blind as the LORD's servant? Seeing many things, but thou observest not; opening the ears, but he heareth not. The LORD is well pleased for his righteousness' sake; he will magnify the law and make it honourable', Isaiah 42:19-21.

Though men might call him blind, yet he was perfect, and seeing many things. Who is deaf as my messenger? opening the ears, but thou hearest not. Though he was blind, yet he saw many things; and though he was deaf, yet he opened the ears of others.

And one of the many things, which the Lord's perfect messenger saw, was the day of Jerusalem's destruction; and this he declared eight or nine hundred years before it came to pass. 'I have trodden the winepress alone, and of the people there was none with me. For I will tread them in mine anger, and trample them in my fury, and their blood shall be sprinkled upon my garments, and I will stain all my raiment. For the day of vengeance is in mine heart, and the year of my redeemed is come.'

The day of vengeance, that was in his heart, was the day of Jerusalem's destruction: 'Let not them that are in the countries enter into the city; for these be the days of vengeance', Luke 21:21,22. The year of his redeemed was not the year in which Christ died, when he redeemed his elect from death and hell; but the time of the saints' redemption from Jewish persecution. 'And when these things begin to come to pass, then look up, and lift up your heads, for your redemption draweth nigh', Luke 21:28.

Christ redeems his people from the deceit and violence of men, as well as from the wrath of God; 'And precious shall their blood be in his sight', Psalm 72:14. And so the Jews found it when all the righteous blood shed, from the blood of Abel to Zacharias, was required of that generation.

The going forth of the commandment to build Jerusalem, and from that time to the coming of Messiah the prince, and to the cutting off the Messiah; and the people of the Roman prince that was to come to Jerusalem to destroy the city and the sanctuary; together with the seven years' peace with many nations, which the Romans were to make during the time of their war with the Jews till God's decreed indignation was poured out upon the desolate; were all foretold by the angel Gabriel to Daniel, Daniel 9:25-28. And the whole of this matter was made known to Gabriel by a man clothed in linen, which was no other than the high priest of our profession. 'And I heard a man's voice between the banks of Ulai, which called, and said, Gabriel, make this man to understand the vision', Daniel 8:16.

Hence it appears that, though he knew not that woeful day as man, yet he knew it as God, and highly resented their cruel treatment of him, and their blasphemy against his Holy Spirit; for it was Christ that executed that fearful judgment upon them, God having committed all judgment to the Son, and all power in heaven and on earth. And he displayed it with a witness, as he foretold them he would; 'Yea, mine own familiar friend in whom I trusted, which did eat of my bread, hath lifted up his heel against me. But thou, O LORD, be merciful unto me, and raise me up, that I may requite them', Psalm 41:9,10.

And he did requite them: for it was he that mustered the Roman army, and brought it against them: and the appearance of that was the sign of the Son of man in heaven, when all the tribes of the earth were to mourn, Mt. 24:30.

The Jews had long required of him a sign from heaven, and he gave them one. The destruction and desolation of the Jews was not to come till Messiah was cut off; and their ruin and destruction was a sure sign that Jesus was the Messiah; and, though the blind Jews could not see it, the children of light did.

These, my dearly beloved, are the men that labour at Zion's foundation, which to them is a stumblingstone and a rock of offence; and too often do they prevail, till the foundations are almost hid, and then God raiseth up others to bring them forth again. 'And they that shall be of thee shall build the old waste places: thou shalt raise up the foundations of many generations; and thou shalt be called, The repairer of the breach, The restorer of paths to dwell in', Isa. 58:12. Thus some bring to light, and some bury; some pull down, and some build up. 'He that is not with me is against me, and he that gathereth not with me, scattereth.'

the eighth meditation

VIII

The Eighth Meditation

I SHALL now resume my former subject, namely, the unctuous experience which believers have of the glorious mystery occupying our meditation.

I showed in a former epistle that if ever our hearts were comforted, if they were ever knit together in love, and if ever we come to the full assurance of understanding, it must be by a humble 'acknowledgement of the mystery of God, and of the Father, and of Christ; in whom are hid all the treasures of wisdom and knowledge', Col. 2:2,3.

This mystery is not only to be acknowledged or assented to as a revealed truth, but it is to be embraced by faith, and to be held, and held fast, as many violent and unwearied attacks, both by devils and heretics, will be made against it. For if we are unsound or unsettled in the groundwork or foundation, all the rest will be out of order. The building cannot be fitly framed, according to the account of a wise master-builder, unless the glorious householder be savingly known; for it is a mystical building, founded in faith, and cemented together in love, and grows up in wisdom, knowledge, and power, not by human might nor by the power of free-will, but by my Spirit, saith the Lord of hosts.

Take the apostle's account; 'Now, therefore, ye are no more strangers and foreigners, but fellow citizens with the saints and of the household of God; and are built upon the foundation of the apostles and prophets, Jesus Christ himself being the chief corner stone; in whom all the building, fitly framed together, groweth unto an holy temple in the Lord; in whom ye also are builded together for an habitation of God through the Spirit', Eph. 2:19-22. The apostle tells us that the living stones, the choice materials of this building, are God's household, freeborn citizens; and that Jesus Christ is the chief corner stone that unites all saints, Jews and Gentiles, together; and that the building grows up into an holy temple in the Lord, an habitation of God through the Spirit.

If the Son of God be left out of our faith, there is no foundation; and if God the Father, or the Holy Spirit, be left out, where is the inhabitant? It is an habitation of God through the Spirit. Christ is the nearest object to faith, as our mediator. 'Ye believe in God, believe also in me'; for through Christ we believe in God, who raised him from the dead, I Peter 1:21. And we receive the promise of the Spirit through faith. Here is the mystery; faith lays hold of Jesus Christ, and through him we believe in God the Father, and, upon our believing, we receive the Spirit, and are sealed by him.

This is the groundwork, the basis, and power, on which faith stands or rests; all building is in vain without this. 'Building up yourselves upon your most holy faith, praying in the Holy Ghost, keep yourselves in the love of God, looking for the mercy of our Lord Jesus Christ unto eternal life.' The most Holy Trinity is the mystery on which faith rests; and we stand by faith, or rest on the powerful confidence which the arm of God reveals in us. Hence the exhortation, 'Hold the mystery of faith in a pure conscience', I Tim. 3:9.

This is called building up ourselves on our most holy faith. Faith is the Father's gift to us through Christ, and from his fulness it comes, and by the operation of the Spirit it is wrought in us, and therefore called a fruit of the Spirit; this is the basis, namely, the Holy Trinity. Love is the bond of union, or the grand cement that compacts and builds up; charity edifieth, or raises the edifice. Hence we read of the love of God to us in giving the Son; and the love of the Son, in laying down his life for us; and the love of the Holy Ghost also. 'Now I beseech you, for the Lord Jesus Christ's sake, and for the love of the Spirit', Rom. 15:30.

The love of the Trinity to us is the bond of union, which, when perceived by faith, and enjoyed, leads to a most blessed freedom and familiarity with the Father, Son, and Spirit; as you read, 'And to make all men see what is the fellowship of the mystery', Eph. 3:9. We can have fellowship with nothing but persons; there is no fellowship with names. These things have I written unto you, that you may have fellowship with us; and truly our fellowship is with the Father, and with his Son Jesus Christ. And you read of the comfort of love, and of the fellowship of the Spirit, Phil. 2:1.

Hence the foundation of vital godliness is God—Father, Son, and Spirit. Faith apprehends this, and by a full persuasion stays the mind thereon; love is the cementing bond that unites the soul to God. 'He that loveth dwelleth in God, and God in him'; that is, he abideth in the Trinity; he abideth in the Son, and in the Father. And it is added, 'As that anointing hath taught you, you shall abide in him.' Read I John 2:27. Here is our inbeing and abiding in the Father, Son, and Spirit; and fellowship is the effect of this union.

True fellowship among men is a company of real friends meeting together in love. 'God was in Christ reconciling the world to himself.' 'When we were enemies, we were reconciled to God by the death of his Son.' And the Holy Ghost applies the word of reconciliation. 'Henceforth I call you not servants; for the servant knoweth not what his lord doeth: but I have called you friends; for all things that I have heard of my Father I have made known unto you', John 15:15.

Persons in fellowship often meet and associate together. Believers, with their confessions, prayers, praises, and thank-offerings, pay their constant visits to their God: and in their conclusive doxologies address all the three divine Persons distinctly; and by these we ascend, in faith and affection, to the Almighty. And, with respect to the sensible enjoyment of God's presence, the Holy Trinity condescends to abide with us. 'If a man love me, he will keep my words: and my Father will love him, and we will come unto him, and make our abode with him', John 14:23. And the Holy Ghost comes also; 'The Comforter, whom I will send unto you from the Father.' Thus does the holy and blessed Trinity visit and take up his abode with believing souls.

Persons in real union and fellowship are a comfort to each other, and partake of each other's joys. 'And I will pray the Father, and he shall give you another Comforter, that he may abide with you for ever', John 14:16. Christ does not say, I myself will pray to myself, that I may send myself; which would have been the right way of expressing the matter, if there were but one Person in the Trinity: but, 'I will pray the Father.' Here is Christ upon earth praying; the Father in heaven prayed unto; and another Comforter, distinct from two divine Persons, prayed for.

The Father comforts us by revealing his dear Son in us, and by accepting us in the Beloved, and appearing well pleased with us in his righteousness. 'And in that day thou shalt say, O

Lord, I will praise thee; though thou wast angry with me, thine anger is turned away, and thou comfortest me', Isa. 12:1.

The Saviour comforts us by speaking the word of eternal life to our hearts. 'The words that I speak unto you, they are spirit, and they are life.' 'My sheep hear my voice, and I know them, and they follow me: and I give unto them eternal life; and they shall never perish, neither shall any pluck them out of my hand', John 10:27,28. 'This is my comfort in my affliction: for thy word hath quickened me', Psalm 119:50.

The Holy Spirit comforts us, by applying the promises to us, and attending them with power; the word comes with power in the Holy Ghost, and in much assurance; which power brings peace, joy, and gladness of heart; which is called the sincere milk of the word; and so it is written, 'Rejoice with Jerusalem, and be glad with her, all ye that love her: rejoice for joy with her, all ye that mourn for her: that ye may suck, and be satisfied with the breasts of her consolations; that ye may milk out, and be delighted with the abundance of her glory. For thus, saith the LORD, Behold, I will extend peace to her like a river, and the glory of the Gentiles like a flowing stream: then shall ye suck, ye shall be borne upon her sides, and be dandled upon her knees. As one whom his mother comforteth, so will I comfort you; and ye shall be comforted in Jerusalem', Isa. 66:10-13.

This joy, consolation, love, and peace, are in the new testament called the fruits of the Spirit, Gal. 5:22.

Persons in true fellowship have great confidence in each other, and know much of each other's minds; and so it is with God and his saints. In the saints' worst hours they believe without doubting the truth of God, and the truth of the whole of his word; whether they can take the comfort of it or not, they know it is true, and that God, the author of it, is true: and, as God is true, so he makes his children sound in the truth, lovers of it, and earnest contenders for it, and sworn enemies to all false doctrines. 'For he said, Surely they are my people, children that will not lie; so he was their Saviour.'

They know much of each other's minds; and so it is with God and his elect: they are made acquainted with God the Father's secret purposes of grace, of his counsels and his covenant, of his good will of purpose and of promise in Christ Jesus before the world began. Christ chooses us out of the world, and discovers himself to us, with all his finished work and saving benefits; while the Holy Spirit takes of the things that are his, and shows them to us, and makes them manifest in our hearts, and secretly seals us up to the day of redemption.

Persons in fellowship often feast and banquet together. The Father makes us a feast of fat things, of marrow and fatness, and of wines on the lees well refined, Isa. 25:6. Which glorious feast is the offering up of Christ, in sacrifice, once for us all. This is bringing forth the fatted calf to entertain the returning prodigals. Wisdom says, 'She hath killed her beasts; she hath mingled her wine; she hath furnished her table. Come, eat of my bread, and drink of the wine which I have mingled', Prov. 9:2,5.

And no sooner does the poor perishing sinner's mind and conscience feast upon his sin-atoning blood and life-giving flesh, but the fire of inbred lusts, the fiery wrath of a broken law, and the fiery darts of Satan are all quenched and dispersed, while the Holy Spirit and his grace flow in, and overshadow the soul with the discovery of Christ, as the end of the law for righteousness. 'I sat down under his shadow with great delight, and his fruit was sweet to my taste', Song 2:3.

And, as the Almighty banquets us, so does he feast and feed upon the satisfaction Christ made for sin, and upon the fruits of his own implanted grace. 'But the Father said to his servants, Bring forth the best robe, and put it on him; and put a ring on his hand, and shoes on his feet: and bring hither the fatted calf, and kill it; and let us eat, and be merry', Luke 15:22,23.

And the Saviour says, 'I am come into my garden, my sister, my spouse: I have gathered my myrrh with my spice; I have eaten my honeycomb with my honey; I have drunk my wine with my milk: eat, O friends; drink, yea, drink abundantly, O beloved', Song 5:1.

Nor is the Holy Spirit less entertained, when we are lively under his influence, observant of his instructions, and obedient to his dictates; as appears by the approbation that he gives, the witness that he bears to our hearts, and by filling us with more of his grace, while we are blessing him for what we have already received.

When the apostles were apprehended and taken before the council of the Jews, and threatened and charged to teach no more in the name of Jesus, the Spirit of God enabled them to speak with such fortitude that the council marvelled; and, when they joined their own company, and put up their united prayers, the Holy Spirit shook the very house, and filled them all again. 'And when they had prayed, the place was shaken where they were assembled together; and they were all filled with the Holy Ghost, and they spake the word of God with boldness', Acts 4:31.

For, as the Spirit is said to be grieved by the sins of some men, and to be vexed and rebelled against by others; so he rejoices in some, approves of others, and fortifies them to the astonishment of their most inveterate persecutors.

Philip, when he obeyed the Spirit's voice, and joined himself to the Ethiopian's chariot, and preached Jesus to him, was caught away by the Spirit of the Lord, and was found at Azotus, Acts 8:39,40. He fortified, furnished, and emboldened Paul before the Roman governor, that Felix trembled when Paul stood undaunted. He made Stephen's face shine like the face of an angel, when his persecutors gnashed their teeth with anguish and desperation; and made Paul and Silas sing the high praises of God in the prison at midnight; and sent an earthquake and shook the prison to the foundation thereof, and opened the doors of it, and made the chains fall from off the criminals, to let them know that he proclaims liberty to captives: 'For where the Spirit of the Lord is, there is liberty'; and this the poor jailor found soon after to his astonishment.

In all these things it is easy to see how the Holy Spirit is entertained, pleased and delighted, when men obey his dictates, and give themselves up to be led by him.

Persons in fellowship are jointly engaged: so God and his people are engaged in one cause, and jointly concerned in one interest. God is the portion of his people, and Jacob is the lot of God's inheritance. He that toucheth the saints toucheth the apple of God's eye, and the saints hate them that hate God, and count them their enemies; they love them that love the Lord; and, when any professors turn their backs and forsake God, as Judas did, the real saints always forsake them.

God's own glory, in all his works, is what the saints aim at; and in the defence of God's glory and honour are his people engaged. God seeks a quarrel with the Philistines, and Samson will fight it out if he die in the field. God will avenge his people on the Egyptians, and Moses engages the whole nation.

The wicked Jews judged and condemned the Son of God, and the apostles got upon twelve thrones to judge and condemn them; and when they had passed the sentence upon them the Lord executed it. 'But, when they persecute you in this city, flee ye to another: for verily I say unto you, Ye shall not have gone over the cities of Israel till the Son of man be come', Mt. 10:23.

The world, the flesh and the devil, are God's enemies; and against these do the saints cry, pray, and fight, all their days; and, if they are foiled or overcome, it is called violence, captivity, or a rape, which God will highly resent; and, if they are pressed beyond measure, and despair even of life, and are thrown seven times, and complain, 'I die daily', or, 'For thy sake we are killed all the day long'; yet they up and at it again, and never give over, nor give up, till they die; for, 'As he is, so are we in this world.'

'God so loved the world that he gave his only begotten Son, that we might live through him': and Christ loved the church, and gave himself for it. And the Spirit's love appears in his convincing us of sin, righteousness and judgment; and in taking up his eternal abode with us, when we are the most vile, filthy, and abominable creatures, and to every good work reprobate.

The saints have suffered all sorts of torments, and every kind of death, that men or devils could invent, rather than dishonour their God, or lose their exceeding great reward: hence they labour after conformity to him, and disallow of every lust and corruption that resists his sovereign will.

If God arraign, they will not excuse; if he punish, they accept. If he search, they hide not; if he condemn, they will not acquit; if he rebuke with fire, they approach the light; if he is wroth, they fear and quake; if he invite, they come up; if he chasten, they submit; if he attract, they follow on; if he frown, then they fear; if he command, they commend; if he forbid, they forbear; if he withdraw, they despond; if he threaten, they contract; if he allure, they enlarge; if he is absent, they are jealous; if he indulge, they make free; if his anger burn, they are mute; if he resist, they withdraw; he hides himself, they go in search; his bowels move, their bowels yearn; if he contend, they attend; if kindness flow, their spirits melt; if he forgive, they cannot forget; if he commune, their heart will burn; if he embrace, they swoon in love; if he bind, they will not be free; if he pull down, they will not build up; if he should wound, none else shall heal; if he lay on, they will not throw off; if he detain, none shall release; if he afflict, they will not be soothed; if he shut up, they will not come out; if he desert, they will not be wooed; if he cause grief, they will not hear peace; and, if he chide, they will not flee; he bends his bow, they yield their breast; if he delay, they still persist; if he deny, they will not give up; he will not relieve, they still entreat; he says 'Begone', they importune; he shuts the door, they knock the more.

The divine and essential Word has taken our nature into God; and there is a divine nature lodged in all the saints, and no separation can be made, either by life or by death. O ye saints, my mouth is opened to you, my heart is enlarged; ye are not straitened in me, but in your own bowels. Now for a recompense in the same, I speak as to beloved children, be ye also enlarged. Adieu. Be strong in the grace that is in Christ Jesus, and endure hardness as good soldiers. The Captain has overcome the world, and the victory is yours.

the ninth meditation

IX

The Ninth Meditation

I AM glad that the saints approve, and that anything clear, harmonious, consistent, informing, or establishing, appears to them in my meditations. I shall, therefore, propose to bring forth what remains on my mind, or may yet occur on the sublime subject.

Reason, or the dim light of nature, is a poor guide in this mystery. Light in the head, without love and reverence in the heart, has a tendency to exalt. 'Knowledge puffeth up, but charity edifieth.' A high look, a stiff neck, and a proud heart God will not suffer; but he will dwell with the humble and the contrite, and will own and acknowledge those that reverence, love, and fear him. In his light we see light; and if teachable and tractable, he will guide us with his eye, and lead us by his Spirit; while the inward anointing, which is the illuminating, renewing, softening, and humbling influences of his grace and Holy Spirit, which the saints experience, will teach them all things necessary to be known, or essential to salvation.

The indwelling of the Holy Spirit, and our unctuous experience of his divine impressions and influence, must regulate all our views, opinions, and conclusions upon divine subjects. Whatever the understanding discovers, and the mind conceives, is always handed down to the soul's experience of divine power; the Spirit's work on the soul being an exact and an infallible copy of the revealed mind and will of God in the scriptures of truth; on which account the church is called the pillar and ground of the truth, I Tim. 3:15.

The Spirit is the author of the scriptures, both of the old testament and the new. The gospel is the ministry of the Spirit, II Cor. 3:6. And the Spirit of Christ in the prophets of the old testament, testified beforehand of the sufferings of Christ, and of the glory that should follow, I Pet. 1:11. And we are told that, 'The testimony of Jesus is the spirit of prophecy.'

Therefore, whatever the enlightened understanding discovers, and the mind perceives or conceives, it is immediately handed down to the experience of the Spirit's teaching within to see if it be consistent with the anointing which teacheth all things.

And, if it agree with the anointing, and has the sanction of the Holy Spirit, immediately the mind is led to the written word for support and confirmation, and the Spirit brings some word home to the mind which proves and establishes it; and this witness of God is greater than the witness of all the men in the world.

But, if it agree not with the anointing, and if it receive not the Spirit's sanction, nor any word come in to confirm it, it is rejected and cast out, as being contrary to the anointing. 'And ye need not that any man teach you: but as the same anointing teacheth you', I John 2:27.

Whatsoever, therefore, contradicts the Spirit's work and his teaching is to be rejected. If the saints will attentively observe this inward teaching, they will perceive something of it all the day long; and, without this divine compass, it is in vain to launch out into the profound depths of divine mysteries, and especially that of the Holy Trinity. 'Canst thou by searching find out God? canst thou find out the Almighty unto perfection? The measure thereof is longer than the earth, and broader than the sea', Job 11:7,9. 'Secret things belong unto the LORD our God: but those things which are revealed belong unto us and to our children for ever', Deut. 29:29.

And God has promised that he will give us a heart to know him, for he will pardon them whom he reserves. And again, 'For all shall know me, from the least to the greatest. For I will be merciful to their unrighteousness, and their sins and their iniquities will I remember no more', Heb. 8:11,12. I was led into the glorious mystery of the Holy Trinity by the teaching of God in my own soul. It is written in the prophets, 'All thy children shall be taught of God.' This passage our Lord quotes, 'It is written in the prophets, and they shall be all taught of God. Every man, therefore, that hath heard, and hath learned of the Father, cometh unto me.' And it is added, 'No man can come to me, except the Father, which hath sent me, draw him', John 6:44,45.

Now, from this divine teaching there is none of God's elect exempted; they shall be all taught of God. And the Saviour informs us, that, by God here, God the Father is meant; and he adds, 'Every man, therefore, that hath heard, and hath learned of the Father, cometh unto me.' He must both hear and learn of the Father before he comes to Christ; nor can any man come to Christ except the Father draw him; and all such, says Christ, 'I will raise up at the last day.' From hence we learn that all the elect are taught of the Father; and that all of the Father's pupils come to Christ; and, without being drawn by the Father, they cannot come; and those that do come shall infallibly be saved and raised up at the last day.

But then where is the Father's teaching described? How does he teach us? And what do we hear and learn of him? This is what I will endeavour to make plain. 'The LORD knoweth the thoughts of man, that they are vanity. Blessed is the man whom thou chastenest, O LORD, and teachest him out of thy law; that thou mayest give him rest from the days of adversity, until the pit be digged for the wicked', Psalm 94:11-13.

Now the schoolmaster, by which God teaches us, is the moral law; as for the ceremonial law, that was never enjoined to the Gentiles. Out of this law are we taught of God the Father; and our lessons are prefaced with his chastening rod, 'Blessed is the man whom thou chastenest, and teachest': and Christ says, we both hear and learn of the Father.

Two things we hear; first, the chastening rod. 'The LORD's voice crieth unto the city, and the man of wisdom shall see thy name: hear ye the rod, and who hath appointed it', Micah 6:9. Here is the voice of the Lord crying to the chosen, calling the city of Zion; and here is a rod that speaks, 'Hear ye the rod.' Now this is what our Lord says; we hear, and we learn of the Father; and he teacheth us out of the law.

The second sound that we hear is called the Lord's voice, that cries to the city; and that voice is, by Paul, called a voice of words; it is blackness and darkness, and tempest; the sound of a trumpet, and the voice of words, Heb. 12:18,19. A voice of words, not a life-giving power. And this voice of words is called a killing letter, or the letter that killeth, which, when it came to Paul, sin revived, and he died. And what can kill us, but the curse, or sentence, of the ministration of death, engraven on tables of stone?

The voice we hear, therefore, is the curse of the broken law condemning us; the rod that we hear is the wrath and anger of

God smiting, reproving, and rebuking us. This is what we hear; and the lessons we learn are, the guilt and filth of sin, the wrath of God, and the enmity of our own hearts.

The next lessons we learn are, the holiness, justice, and terrible majesty of God. These are the things that we hear and learn of the Father; and, 'Every one that hath heard and learned of the Father', says Christ, 'cometh unto me'.

Now what is that which is promised to this blessed man, thus chastened and taught out of the law? Why, God will give him rest from the days of adversity, until the pit be digged for the wicked. The thing promised is rest; but who wants rest? None but those who labour, and are heavy laden. The labourer is he who is toiling under the curse and wrath of God, to recommend himself to God's favour, and to get life by the works of the law: and hard labour this is. The load that he carries is the guilt he has contracted, and the corruptions of his heart which the law discovers; and this is a sore burden, too heavy for any to bear.

Now there is a voice in the word to such souls pointing to Christ, 'To whom he said, This is the rest wherewith ye may cause the weary to rest; and this is the refreshing', Isa. 28:12. The Saviour calls to such souls also; 'Come unto me, all ye that labour and are heavy laden, and I will give you rest.' But no invitations will do for a poor soul that finds himself condemned already. And, therefore, 'No man can come to me', says Christ, 'except the Father draw him.'

However, to Christ all that are taught of God must come; for the Spirit of God and the promise of life are both in him; and into his hands are all the elect put, and to his foot they must be brought, and be made to hear his voice, and receive the word from his mouth, that they may live. The fiery law comes first to condemn us to death, and the voice and word of the Son of God afterward to raise the dead. 'The Lord came from Sinai, and rose up from Seir unto them; he shined forth from mount Paran, and he came with ten thousands of saints: from his right hand went a fiery law for them. Yea, he loved the people; all his saints are in thy hand: and they sat down at thy feet; every one shall receive of thy words', Deut. 33:2,3.

This passage shows that all whom the Father teaches out of the fiery law must come to Christ the great prophet, and sit down at his feet to receive of his word. This was the good part which Mary chose that could not be taken from her. Here Mary Magdalene sat, and got her pardon and her much love; and here God draws us all. But how does he draw us?

Firstly, by causing the storms of Sinai now and then to abate, and the arrows of his quiver to lose their keenness.

Secondly, by guiding our eyes to the promises, encouragements, invitations, and kind words spoken by the Lord Jesus.

Thirdly, by causing now and then a ray of light, a beam of hope, and some expectations, to spring up in our hearts while we attend to the voice of Christ in the gospel.

Fourthly, the dreadful passages of scripture that pierced us through get out of sight, and nothing but Christ and his kind dealings with sinners appear; and while our face is turning to the Lord the veil is gradually taken away. The more we see of Jesus, the softer our souls get, and the more our hearts melt; and the more Christ shines in the word, the more we wonder, till his very name appears as a healing ointment poured forth; and, as the bowels yearn over him, so faith in him springs up;

the Holy Spirit then testifies of him, and presents him to view, till the understanding becomes susceptible of the light of his countenance, and confidence goes out and embraces him; then God accepts us in the beloved, and gives us the light of the knowledge of his glory in the face of Jesus Christ, while the Spirit fills us with joy and peace.

And here the soul finds rest from the days of adversity, till the pit be digged up for the wicked; that is, they shall rest safe and secure in Christ Jesus, while the wicked fill up their own measure; for the wicked are said to dig their own pit, and to fall into their own destruction.

This is what the apostle calls coming to God the Judge of all; and to Jesus, the mediator of the new covenant, and to the blood of sprinkling that speaks better things than that of Abel, Heb. 12:23,24. This is a saving and an experimental knowledge of the holy and blessed Trinity. We come first to God in a fiery law; when he chastens and judges us, that we should not be condemned with the world, I Cor. 11:32; and then draws us to Christ, and accepts us in him. And in Jesus Christ we find rest from both our labour and our load, and, at the same time, we come into the glorious liberty of the children of God. The Holy Ghost sheds abroad the love of God in our heart, and this casts out wrath, which is a spirit of bondage to fear, and all torment with it, operating in us as a spirit of love, of power, and of a sound mind.

This is an experimental knowledge of the Holy Trinity, and such as none ever experience but the elect of God; and in this way they are all taught of God; and the experience of this good work is such as Satan and all his emissaries can never destroy. No man thus made wise to salvation, ever dared to set his mouth against the Holy Trinity; and a fool cannot, for this wisdom is too high for him.

This is coming to God, 'The fountain of living waters', Jer. 2:13; and to Christ, the well of salvation, Isaiah 12:3; and to the river, 'The streams whereof make glad the city of God', Ps. 46:4.

Thus, also, saith God: 'I will put my law in their inward parts, and write it in their hearts; and I will be their God, and they shall be my people', Jer. 31:33. 'And I', saith the Saviour, 'will write upon him the name of my God, and the name of the city of my God, which is new Jerusalem, which cometh down out of heaven from my God: and I will write upon him my new name', Rev. 3:12. And the Spirit makes us living epistles; 'Ye are manifestly declared to be the epistle of Christ ministered by us, written not with ink, but with the Spirit of the living God; not in tables of stone, but in fleshy tables of the heart', II Cor. 3:3.

The voice of God the Father's love in the heart is, 'Yea, I have loved thee with an everlasting love; therefore with lovingkindness have I drawn thee.'

The voice of the atonement of Christ, in the believer's conscience, is, pardon, peace and reconciliation with God. And these are better things than those spoken by the blood of Abel, Heb. 12:24.

And the distinct voice of the Holy Ghost in the hearts of all believers is, 'Abba, Father', Gal. 4:6. This divine teaching is attended with a holy claim upon God as our own God; and God will own and acknowledge such. To these God speaks, 'Thou shalt call me, My Father, and thou shalt not turn away from me'; which is what no man can do, in truth, without the witness and voice of the Spirit of adoption; for it is he that cries, Abba, Father. Such souls, also, claim Jesus for their own, with an infallible witness in their own souls of the truth of it; which no man can do, in truth, without the Spirit of God; for, 'No man can say that Jesus is the Lord (with application) but by the Holy Ghost', I Cor. 12:3.

Hence it is plain that the Spirit of God makes us, as he did the prodigal, arise and go to our Father; which, when spoken by the Spirit, is what God will ever own and honour, as he did in that parable; 'This is my son'. And, though at times unbelief prevails, yet the Spirit subdues it again and again, as he did in Thomas, 'My Lord and my God!' These plain truths clearly reveal this most sublime mystery, and these things the children of God have in their own experience; and it is such experience as this that worketh hope.

This is submitting to divine revelation, and not being wise above what is written. And whatever appears dark to us in the word of God we must pray the Lord to shine upon it, that we may know the mind of the Spirit in it; for it is in his light that we see light. And, 'If any man lack wisdom, let him ask of God, who giveth liberally and upbraideth not'; and he will guide us by his counsel.

But let us for ever shun the bold intrusions of unhumbled and unsanctified men, who are so daring and presumptuous; for God will resist such, and make their feet stumble upon the dark mountains; while, 'The meek he will guide in judgment, the meek will he teach his way.' Strange notions are daily circulated in town against these things; and such men shall wax worse and worse, deceiving and being deceived; for, if the force of truth beat them out of one refuge of lies, the devil drives them into another; and, being hardened to the last degree, they can adopt words which one dare not recite, and use arguments which it is scandalous to recount: but the time will come when God will cause the arrogancy of the proud to cease, and will lay low the haughtiness of the terrible, Isa. 13:11.

I shall conclude this long epistle with the triune benediction of heaven. 'The grace of the Lord Jesus Christ, and the love of God, and the communion of the Holy Ghost, be with you', and with all that love our Lord Jesus Christ, now and for evermore.

the tenth meditation

X

The Tenth Meditation

BELOVED, when I finished my ninth epistle I thought I had nearly exhausted the treasure that was to be brought forth upon the present subject. I went last night to my bed weary, having sat hard at it for fifteen hours; and I thought the spring in my heart, as well as my bodily strength, were both spent.

But before I could get to sleep another branch of the matter sprang up, and soon my cup overflowed again, which kept me awake for some time: nor could all my weariness and heaviness counterbalance it, so as to convey me into the regions of forgetfulness. The subject of my contemplation was communion; and here another field opened, and, on entering, this soon became a vast expanse.

The first thing that struck me was the word of God to Moses, 'Thou shalt make a mercy seat of pure gold; and thou shalt make two cherubims of gold, of beaten work shalt thou make them, in the two ends of the mercy seat. And thou shalt put the mercy seat above upon the ark; and in the ark thou shalt put the testimony that I shall give thee. And there I will meet with thee, and I will commune with thee from above the mercy seat', Exodus 25. I knew the mercy seat to be a throne of grace; 'A glorious high throne from the beginning is the place of our sanctuary', Jer. 17:12.

The great condescension of God the Father, which appeared in the above passage, forcibly struck me; the mercy seat I considered to be a type of Christ, who is our throne of grace. He is a father to the inhabitants of Jerusalem, and a glorious throne to his Father's house, Isa. 22:23. The two tables of the testimony were to be put into the ark, so that they were not to terrify nor arrest those that fled for mercy; this led me to the words of Christ, namely, 'Yea, thy law is within my heart; I delight to do thy will, O my God.'

I then considered the words of the psalmist which say, Though the Lord be high, yet hath he respect to the lowly; he humbleth himself to behold the things that are in heaven and in earth, Psalm 113:6. But how much more to meet and commune with men!

To Christ Jesus, who received the sure mercies of David for us, and in whom all the fulness of grace dwells, and who is full of grace and truth, must we poor sinners go, that we may find grace and strength to help in every time of need. And here God promises to meet with us; for Christ is the way to the Father: 'Thou meetest him that rejoiceth, and worketh righteousness, those that remember thee in thy ways.'

I then considered what were the blessed effects of this communion, or what was to be communicated to the children of Israel when God met them in their representative above the mercy seat, and what they were to communicate to him. They were to communicate their troubles, cares, burdens, wants, fears, requests, carrying them to the Lord by prayer, and likewise their recitals of his favours with thanks, praises, blessings, and grateful acknowledgments of them; these were some of the things that they were to communicate to God. And God promises to communicate the following blessings to them by the priest 'The LORD bless thee, and keep thee: the LORD make his face shine upon thee, and be gracious unto thee: the LORD lift up his countenance upon thee, and give thee peace. And they shall put my name upon the children of Israel; and I will bless them.'

This whole cluster of blessings is now to be found in Christ; the blessing of eternal life is in him; we are in his hand, and kept by his power through faith; the knowledge of the glory of God is in the face of Jesus Christ; from his fulness all grace is received, he is the Sun of Righteousness that rises and shines upon us, and he is our peace, who hath made both one, and broken down the middle wall of partition between Jew and Gentile. These were my thoughts of God our heavenly Father communing with us upon the mercy seat.

My mind then considered the free and friendly communion which our Lord Jesus Christ held with Abraham, when he communicated to him his mind and will with respect to the cities of the plain, and how freely Abraham communicated the desires of his soul to the Saviour; all which was granted as long as Abraham could find a heart to ask; and when Abraham stopped in asking, the Lord stopped granting. 'And the LORD went his way as soon as he had left communing with Abraham: and Abraham returned unto his place', Gen. 18:33.

Then my mind passed to the two disciples going to Emmaus. 'And while they communed together Jesus himself drew near, and went with them, and asked them, What manner of communications are these that ye have one to another, as ye walk, and are sad? They answering him said, Art thou only a stranger in Jerusalem, and hast not known the things which are come to pass there in these days? And he said unto them, What things? And they said unto him, Concerning Jesus of Nazareth, which was a prophet mighty in deed and word before God and all the people: and how the chief priests and our rulers delivered him to be condemned to death, and have crucified him. But we trusted that it had been he which should have redeemed Israel. And, beside all this, today is the third day since these things were done. Yea, and certain women also of our company made us astonished, which were early at the sepulchre: and, when they found not his body, they came, saying, That they had also seen a vision of angels, which said that he was alive', Luke 24:15-23.

Here they communicated to the Lord Jesus their bitter grief and trouble, and that the crucifixion of their dear Lord was the sole cause of all their calamities, and that the women's account from the angels that he was yet alive was good news. But they could receive no comfort from these things, for him they saw not. And now he began and opened up the scriptures concerning his sufferings; and, as they had been eyewitnesses of them, they could compare spiritual things with spiritual, while he opened the prophecies of the things concerning himself.

And, after making himself known to them, he vanished out of their sight. However, all that they desired in this world was now granted them: they saw and knew that he was alive. 'And they said one to another, Did not our heart burn within us, while he talked with us by the way, and while he opened to us the scriptures?' Luke 24:32.

I then thought of what the apostle says of our having the same communion with the Holy Spirit also; 'The grace of our Lord Jesus Christ, and the love of God, and the communion of the Holy Ghost, be with you all. Amen', II Cor. 13:14.

And upon the subject of communion with the Holy Ghost my mind is now led.

Real communion is the blessed effect of vital union. God communicates no spiritual blessings to them who are in fellowship with devils, with the unfruitful works of darkness, with unrighteousness, or with infidels or heretics; For 'he that is joined to the Lord is one spirit' with him. And from this union springs communion; and communion is nothing else but giving and receiving, and is both active and passive: active, in giving or bestowing good things upon others; passive, in receiving good things from others.

Now all real believers are united to, and ingrafted into Christ, as the branch is to the vine; and without continual supplies of life, from the vine to the branch, the branch cannot live, much less be fruitful; it must wither and die away. 'If a man abide not in me he is cast forth as a branch and is withered, and men gather them and they are burned.'

No creature can stand alone; angels could not; Adam could not; Judas could not; no, nor could even Peter, 'Woe to him that is alone when he falleth, for there is not another to help him up.' But, he that 'abideth in me, and I in him, the same bringeth forth much fruit; for without me ye can do nothing.'

No stock in hand will do, however large a portion of the Spirit, as Elijah had; however strong the mountain of prosperity, as David's was; however emboldened and fortified, as Peter thought he was when he promised to face either prison or death: all will soon wither without continual supplies. Elijah fled for his life from the face of Jezebel; God hid his face, and David was troubled; and Peter fell before the face of a servant girl.

Christ is the root both of David and of all believers. We are wild olive branches grafted into the good olive tree, and partake of the root and fatness of the olive tree; and we bear not the root, but the root bears us, Rom. 11:17,18. The life of all trees lies in the root; Christ is our life; and we must live in the root, and the root in us, or there will be no fruit. There are continual communications from the root to the tree, and to every branch of it: let this communication be obstructed, or the union cut off, or the intercourse be stopped up, and the tree will show it as soon as the sun shines upon it.

Nothing less than vital union with the living root, and momentary communications therefrom, can keep us either alive or fruitful. 'In that day sing ye unto her, A vineyard of red wine. I the Lord do keep it, I will water it every moment; lest any hurt it, I will keep it night and day.' Momentary support and supplies, and nothing else, can keep the strongest believer standing; without this all joys, yea, the strongest joys, will wither away from the sons of men, Joel 1:10.

Hence the apostle endeavours to bring his beloved son Timothy off from trusting in his own comfortable frames, however strong they might be, knowing that they are very short lived, transient, and continually changing; 'My son, be strong in the grace that is in Christ Jesus', II Tim. 2:1. Here grace is, in all its fulness, always the same, and inexhaustible; and it is in the fountain, and not in the streams, that we must trust; for even for temporal supplies it will not do to trust in the grist that is in the house, nor in the barn that fills the grist, nor yet in the harvest that fills the barn; but in the living God, who promises seedtime and harvest, and who giveth us richly all things to enjoy, I Tim. 6:17.

But then how are these momentary supplies of life and strength, grace and help, to be communicated to us? I answer, By the Holy Spirit of God. As it is written, 'For I know that this shall turn to my salvation through your prayer, and the supply of the Spirit of Jesus Christ', Phil. 1:19. Again, 'Howbeit, when he the Spirit of truth is come, he will guide you into all truth: for he shall not speak of himself; but whatsoever he shall hear, that shall he speak: and he will show you things to come. He shall glorify me; for he shall receive of mine, and shall show it unto you.'

All spiritual and temporal blessings, truths, promises, grace, and glory, are secured to us in an everlasting covenant; which covenant was ratified and confirmed by the death of Christ, and therefore he is called the covenant: 'I will keep thee, and give thee for a covenant of the people', Isa. 42:6. In him all covenant mercies and blessings are found, and he is appointed the heir of all things, Heb. 1:2; and we are heirs of God, joint heirs with Christ, Rom. 8:17.

The first work of the Holy Spirit is to convince of sin. 'If I go not away the Comforter will not come unto you; but, if I depart, I will send him unto you. And, when he is come, he will reprove (or convince) the world of sin', John 16:7,8. Sometimes the Holy Spirit sends the word with such force and terrible majesty, as to arm the conscience of a sinner with a troop of terrors against him; which stops the mouth even of a gainsayer, and makes the preacher manifest in the conscience even of a persecutor; and yet does not convert him, nor bring him to the light, but so silences him that even such an enemy is made to live in peace with a man whose ways have pleased God, Prov. 16:7.

But, when the Holy Spirit comes to convince a chosen vessel of sin, he applies the truth with such a piercing power as to penetrate into the deep recesses of the heart, which alarms and awakens the conscience; this is followed up with continual reproofs and rebukes; and he attends all his reproofs and rebukes with divine light, which makes the sinner's crimes manifest, and lays them all open to his view, even his secret sins and all his works of darkness: 'For it is a shame even to speak of those things which are done of them in secret. But all things that are reproved are made manifest by the light: for whatsoever doth make manifest is light', Eph. 5:12,13.

No candle ever discovered the foulness of a room, nor the sun in his full strength the dust and atoms that fly in it, as the Holy Spirit discovers the guilt and filth, the corruptions and deceptions, of the human heart; as it is written, 'And it shall come to pass at that time, that I will search Jerusalem with candles, and punish the men that are settled on their lees', Zeph. 1:12. Hence our Lord told the disciples that, 'Men do not light a candle to put it under a bushel.'

And when the Holy Spirit came upon the apostles he searched Jerusalem with a witness; he mightily convinced the Jews of their unbelief, of their persecution, rejection, and crucifixion of Christ; and brought it home to their souls with such infallible proofs and facts as cut them to the heart, and made them cry out, 'Men and brethren, what shall we do?'

And here I can but take notice of a passage in Solomon's Proverbs, which is as real a prophecy, and was as punctually fulfilled in the apostles' days, as any prediction in the bible; and sure I am that the words were spoken by the Spirit of Christ: 'Turn you at my reproof: behold, I will pour out my spirit unto you, I will make known my words unto you', Prov. 1.23. This Peter promised them, 'Repent, and be baptized every one of you, and ye shall receive the gift of the Holy Ghost', Acts 2:38.

And, as Solomon foretold, desolations came upon the rest; 'But ye have set at nought all my counsel, and would none of my reproof: I also will laugh at your calamity; I will mock when your fear cometh; when your fear cometh as desolation, and your destruction cometh as a whirlwind; then shall they call, but I will not answer', Prov. 1:25-28.

The Spirit not only convinces of sin, and gives cutting reproofs and rebukes for it, but he applies the word with power, and fixes it upon the mind; otherwise the elect would be robbed, as the reprobate is, 'then cometh the wicked one, and steals the word sown out of his heart, and he becometh unfruitful.' But the Spirit makes a powerful application of the word to the elect, and by this God gives testimony to the word of his grace.

The Holy Spirit attends the convictions and reproofs that he gives with life, and the quickening influences of the Spirit makes his reproofs sink deep, and this makes the poor sinner's sensations so keen that he cannot rest day nor night: otherwise he would act as did Cain, amusing himself with other things, as he did when he built a city; or like Saul, who sought to the witch of Endor; or like the young man in the gospel, who went away sorrowful, and yet hugged his worldly possessions. But it is not so with a soul convinced by the Holy Spirit; he does not want to shake his convictions off by going from Christ, as the convicted accusers of the adulterous woman did; all his fears are, that his convictions will wear off, and that he shall be given up to his own heart's lust.

But the Holy Spirit makes the heart honest: the convicted soul receives the word in an honest and good heart; and therefore comes to the light, that his deeds may be made manifest that they are wrought in God. His language is, Search me and try me. He accepts the punishment of his iniquity, and would put his mouth in the dust, if so be that there might be hope; he kisses the rod, and dreads the thoughts of carnal ease. He is an enemy of them that would bolster him, or cry, Peace, Peace, or heal his wounds lightly; 'To the hungry soul every bitter thing is sweet.'

He would sooner labour under the guilt of sin, and the wrath of God, than fail of his grace, or be set down short of the promised rest. He sees the deceitfulness of sin, the treachery of his heart, and the cunning of the devil; and trembles at the sentence of the law, and the severity of the Most High. He that rebukes him finds more favour in his eyes than he that flatters with his lips, Prov. 28:23. Sweet to him are the wounds of a friend, but the kisses of an enemy are deceitful, Prov. 27:6.

Thus does the Holy Spirit communicate power, life, honesty, and sincerity, with the convictions and reproofs which he applies to the elect of God.

The Spirit supports them under the burden of sin which they feel, and under the sight of it which he presents to their view, and sustains them under the wrath and curse of a broken law; They are holpen with a little help. Through the fire he is with them, and through the water; or else the former would dry up their spirits, and the latter drown them in desperation.

And in all these things the convinced sinner obeys his divine operator, though he does not know who it is that leads him. The evils which the Holy Spirit discovers to him he confesses; the reproofs he gives he falleth under; to the word the Spirit leads him, and he searches the scriptures daily.

Where he hears the word with power, and where he finds his case pointed out, there the preacher is made manifest in his conscience; there he desires to abide, however searching and trying the ministry may be: for where he gets his wounding there he expects his healing; 'He that is of God heareth God's word. We are of God', says John, 'and he that is of God heareth us; and he that is not of God heareth not us.'

The same Spirit that gives him light and quickening grace sets him to crying to God, 'And I will pour upon the house of David, and upon the inhabitants of Jerusalem, the spirit of grace and of supplications.'

The life and feeling, the holy longings, the desires, thirstings, cravings, and bitter cries, which are found in the convinced sinner, all spring from the energy and operations of the Holy Spirit of God: hence the many precious promises that are held forth in the word of God to such poor souls; 'Shall not God avenge his own elect, which cry day and night?' 'When the poor and needy seek water and there is none, and their tongue fails for thirst, I the Lord will hear them, I the God of Israel will not forsake them.' 'Wait upon God, and he shall give thee the desires of thine heart: trust in him, and he shall bring it to pass.' 'They shall come that are ready to perish.' 'Because of the sighing of the poor, now will I arise, saith the Lord.' 'I will satiate the weary, I will replenish the sorrowful soul, I will pour water on him that is thirsty, and floods upon the dry ground.' 'Blessed are they that hunger and thirst.' ' Blessed are the poor in spirit.'

Again, 'Thou shalt weep no more: he will be very gracious unto thee at the voice of thy cry; when he shall hear it, he will answer thee', Isa. 30:19.

All these intense longings and holy breathings are produced under the quickening energy of the Holy Spirit, even before he proclaims liberty to us, or creates the fruit of the lip, Isa. 57:19; or gives us a door of utterance, Acts 2:4. 'The Spirit itself maketh intercession for us, with groanings which cannot be uttered.'

And this was known by the apostles themselves, before that miraculous out-pouring of the Spirit upon them, on the day of Pentecost. The apostles had felt the power of the Spirit attending the word; 'He spake as one having authority, and not as the scribes'; for, 'his word was with power.' He had convinced them of sin, as may be seen in their different cases, described by our Lord's first sermon on the mount, and by the confession of Peter; 'Depart from me, for I am a sinful man, O Lord.' They owned that Christ had the words of eternal life; yea, and they believed in him; 'Father, the word which thou hast given me I have given them, and they have received it, and have believed that I came forth from thee, and that thou didst send me.'

And they loved him too, and abode with him: and both faith and love are fruits of the Holy Spirit. But, as the Spirit of revelation and understanding, as a distinct Comforter, as the Spirit of power and of a sound mind, with all his miraculous gifts and graces, they were yet to be baptized with him in this wonderful way not many days hence. Hence it is said that, 'The Holy Ghost was not yet given, because that Jesus was not yet glorified.' Power, also, in a wonderful manner, they were to receive when the Holy Ghost came upon them, to embolden them, and enable them to preach the gospel in all languages, and to work miracles in confirmation of it.

I must beg pardon for exceeding the limits of an epistle. When next I have opportunity I shall resume on this divine subject. Meantime, begetting, quickening, travailing, and bringing forth, still go on among us; 'Our bed is green', Song 1:16.

the eleventh meditation

XI

The Eleventh Meditation

THE Holy Spirit testifies of Christ; 'But when the Comforter is come, whom I will send unto you from the Father, even the Spirit of truth, which proceedeth from the Father, he shall testify of me', John 15:26. And this the Holy Spirit does by giving testimony to the word of his grace; by proving the truth and reality of the word to the sensible sinner's conscience; by attending it with light, evidence, and full demonstration; so that Christ is evidently set forth as crucified before the soul, Gal. 3:1. Christ's voice is heard and felt, and his all-subduing power is displayed within.

The Spirit testifies of him as the almighty and eternal God, by the glorious majesty of Christ which the Spirit discovers, and which shines into the heart. 'Arise, shine, for thy light is come, and the glory of God is risen upon thee; and the Lord shall be thine everlasting light, and thy God thy glory.' Under this manifestation the soul falls prostrate before him; owns, honours, adores, and worships him.

The Spirit testifies of him as our high priest, and applies the atonement, with pardon and peace, as the blessed effects of it.

He testifies of him as our physician; and the proof of it is, our iniquities are all forgiven, and all our infirmities are healed.

He testifies of him as the end of the law for righteousness, by applying that righteousness to the heart, and by passing the sentence of justification upon the conscience; at which time Christ, as our advocate, silences all our accusers; and, as our mediator, he gives us access to God, a claim upon him, and boldness with him.

The Holy Spirit testifies of him as our King, and reveals him as such, and erects his empire in the soul upon our reception of Christ; which stands in power, in righteousness, peace, and joy in the Holy Ghost. When sin is dethroned, the devil, his armour, and artillery, are cast out, death is abolished, life and immortality are brought to light, and the fear of death and the dread of damnation are dispersed; and all our perplexing doubts, cares, and gloomy thoughts about it scattered into all winds.

Thus, does the Holy Spirit testify of Christ, and gives evident proofs of his ability to save to the uttermost; he realises his saving benefits, applies his merits, proclaims his omnipotence, his mild and blessed government, the powerful sway of his righteous sceptre, and the glorious majesty of his kingdom.

The application of all the promises is the work of the Holy Spirit. The promise of life and the spirit of life always go together, for it is the powerful application of the word by the Spirit that makes the promise; 'The incorruptible seed, the word of God, that liveth and abideth for ever.' All the promises of divine consolation have their sincere milk from Christ by the Holy Spirit; one promise brings peace, another joy, another love, another comfort, another rest; just as the Holy Spirit sends them in, so they discharge their rich contents: the hungry soul, by exercising faith upon them, sucks the sweetness of them till he is filled with joy unspeakable and full of glory.

'Rejoice ye with Jerusalem, and be glad with her, all ye that love her: rejoice for joy with her, all ye that mourn for her: that ye may suck, and be satisfied with the breasts of her consolations; that ye may milk out, and be delighted with the abundance of her glory', Isa. 66:10,11.

There is no converting, refreshing, encouraging power attends the word without the Spirit's operation. When he makes application of it, faith, life, and love attend it; for, 'Our gospel came not unto you in word only, but in power, and in the Holy Ghost, and in much assurance.'

And various are the sensations of the soul under the Spirit's influence when he applies the word: sometimes it is a word of support that fortifies and strengthens: sometimes a word of encouragement to keep us watching, waiting, and to bear us up under trials and crosses; sometimes a word of correction that leads us to self-examination, which awes us, and excites watchfulness and amendment; at other times a soft word that breaketh the bones, and melts us under a sense of undeserved love and self-abhorrence; and often a word of instruction to correct the mind, disperse some wrong notion, to inform the judgment, and to bring more harmonious and consistent views of things to the soul.

Innumerable are the ways by which the Holy Spirit works by the word, and in his application of it; but it is always a seasonable application; 'And a word spoken in due season, how good is it!' 'A word fitly spoken is like apples of gold in pictures of silver', Prov. 15:23 and 25:11.

The secret things of God, such as his counsel and covenants, are made known to us by the Holy Spirit; 'What man knoweth the things of a man, save the spirit of man which is in him?

even so the things of God knoweth no man, but the Spirit of God', I Cor. 2:11.

The Holy Spirit, when he has testified of Christ to us, leads us back to his great undertaking and appointment from everlasting; he leads us up to the everlasting love of God, and to his absolute choice of us in Christ Jesus: to his secret decrees of election and predestination; to his good will of purpose in Christ, and to the secret counsel of his will; and to his covenant made with Christ before the world began: 'For the froward is abomination to the LORD; but his secret is with the righteous', Prov. 3:32. 'The secret of the Lord is with them that fear him; and he will show them his covenant.'

The secret of predestinating us to the adoption of children by Christ Jesus, and of his giving us life in him, and of his ordaining us to it before the world began, is revealed and made known to the elect of God by the Spirit; and our knowledge of these things, and of our interest in them, is our highest wisdom. 'But we speak the wisdom of God in a mystery, even the hidden wisdom, which God ordained before the world unto our glory: which none of the princes of this world knew: for had they known it, they would not have crucified the Lord of glory. But as it is written, Eye hath not seen, nor ear heard, neither have entered into the heart of man, the things which God hath prepared for them that love him. But God hath revealed them unto us by his Spirit: for the Spirit searcheth all things, yea, the deep things of God', I Cor. 2:7-10.

Our faith is called the faith of God's elect, not only because it is a grace peculiar to them, but because God's election of us is a truth revealed to faith, and a truth which faith apprehends and holds fast; for there can be no such thing as making our calling and election sure, without being assured that there is such a doctrine as election.

From God's secret counsel and covenant springs no small part of our unspeakable joy. God fills us with joy and peace in believing, and especially in believing our election of God; 'Notwithstanding in this rejoice not, that the spirits are subject unto you; but rather rejoice, because your names are written in heaven', Luke 10:20.

If these things are lacking in our faith, our faith is deficient in one of the most sublime and establishing articles. He that believeth the love that God hath to him, is led to believe that this love took its rise from eternity, for there are no new acts in God; and from those ancient settlements are the goings forth of Christ dated. 'But thou, Bethlehem Ephratah, though thou be little among the thousands of Judah, yet out of thee shall he come forth unto me that is to be ruler in Israel; whose goings forth have been from of old, from everlasting', Micah 5:2. Into these deep things does the Holy Spirit lead us, and into a humble acquiescence with them, and fills us with wonder and astonishment at them.

And he likewise leads us into the distinct personal works of the holy and blessed Trinity. As a spirit of adoption he gives us power and boldness to claim our interest in God as our covenant God and Father; 'But as many as received him to them gave he power to become the sons of God, even to them that believe on his name: which were born, not of blood, nor of the will of the flesh, nor of the will of man, but of God.' This birth makes our sonship clear: love gives us a dwelling in God; 'He that loveth dwelleth in God, and God in him.' Faith gives us a dwelling in Christ, 'That Christ may dwell in your hearts by faith.'

And the Spirit's witness proves our adoption, the Spirit cries 'Abba, Father'. Receiving power to become the sons of God, is receiving the Spirit; and by the Spirit the grace of faith, to enable us, as I before observed, with a holy boldness to claim our sonship before God. 'But I said, How shall I put thee among the children, and give thee a pleasant land, a goodly heritage of the hosts of nations? And I said, Thou shalt call me, My father; and shalt not turn away from me', Jer. 3:19.

This promise the Spirit makes good; he makes us say, My father. And this may be seen in the prodigal son, 'I will arise, and go to my father.' These words were spoken under the emboldening and encouraging influence of the Spirit of adoption; and whatever the Holy Spirit says or does is always owned and honoured by God the Father, and confirmed in heaven; as may be seen in that parable: 'This is my son', says God; 'he was dead, and is alive again; he was lost, and is found.'

The Jews spoke the same language the prodigal did, even to Christ; 'We have one Father, even God.' But this is neither owned nor honoured; for, 'If God were your Father', says Christ, 'you would love me: for I proceeded forth and came from God; neither came I of myself, but he sent me. Ye are of your father the devil, and the lusts of your father ye will do. He was a murderer from the beginning, and abode not in the truth, because there is no truth in him', John 8:42,44. Thus we see that no claim upon birth privileges, no, not upon national religion; no unwarrantable, no presumptuous claims upon God, are either approved or confirmed.

The Holy Spirit is given for a witness to us. 'If we receive the witness of men', as many do, and rest in it, 'the witness of God is greater.' 'He that believes hath the witness in himself.' And sure I am, that without the infallible testimony of the Holy Ghost no poor convinced, self-condemned, and self-despairing sinner could ever lay any claim upon the Almighty.

A sensible sinner, who feels the enmity of his mind and the rebellion of his heart, who is loathsome in his own sight, and conscious to himself that he is a child of wrath, and a willing drudge to Satan; for such an one to call God his Father, even while God's wrath and jealousy seem to smoke against him, he would think it the vilest presumption in such a wretch as he, and the greatest affront and insult, the greatest dishonour and indignity, that could be offered to the majesty of heaven; rather, his language is to say to corruption, 'Thou art my father; and to the worm, Thou art my mother', Job 17:14.

But to think that God would, or could, ever acknowledge or accept such an one as a child of his, is what would never have entered his mind world without end, if the Holy Ghost did not put it there. And he does it in the following manner: First, he silences all the sinner's accusers and all accusations, and brings the confused and confounded soul into a state of the most profound calm, quietude, peace and tranquillity.

Here our sins, which appeared like the sins of Sodom, crying to heaven; conscience, also, with his cutting accusations; the law, with all its curses and unlimited demands; justice, with his calls for vengeance; Satan, with all his blasphemies, fiery darts, accusations, and terrible suggestions; together with all our heart-misgivings and heart-risings, and those terrible passages of scripture which describe the fruitless cries of Esau, the horrors of Judas, the misery of Cain, the distraction of Saul, and the fearful end of Korah, Abiram, and Dathan; are all stilled and hushed into the profoundest silence, the violent storm of wrath abates, and the troubled sea ceases from her raging.

The poor sinner stands astonished to know what are become of all his accusers; he looks about him, and finds that all his sins which were set in order against him, all his secret sins which stood in the light of God's countenance, are blotted out as a cloud, and his transgressions as a thick cloud; and, as far as the east is from the west, so far does God separate his transgressions from him. The guilt and filth of sin within is all purged away, and every inbred corruption is subdued and out of sight; so that not one unclean bird remains upon the living sacrifice.

The Holy Spirit sets Christ crucified before the eye of faith; while the Spirit, in the application of the blood of sprinkling, speaks pardon, peace, reconciliation, and perfect friendship. Sin being purged, nothing separates or stands between God and the soul.

The Holy Ghost sheds abroad God's love in the heart, which casts out fear and torment, doubts, and all misgivings of the heart about it; while love dissolves the stony heart, melts the stubborn mind, and makes the rebellious will submit and become pliant. Joy unutterable flows in, while floods of pious and godly sorrow flow out. The benign Father of all mercies, and God of all comfort, indulges the soul with the greatest freedom and familiarity, and with nearness of access to him.

God shines well pleased in the face of Jesus, accepts and embraces the soul in him; while faith, attended with the fullest assurance, springs up and goes forth in the fullest exercise upon the everlasting love of God, and on the finished salvation of Jesus Christ, and is fully persuaded of her eternal interest in both; while the Holy Spirit cries, Abba, Father; to which cry both law and gospel, the love of God and the blood of Christ, retributive justice and honest conscience, all put their hearty Amen.

The Holy Spirit, with the witness that he bears, follows the convinced sinner through every stage of his experience, from his first awakening, until his translation into the kingdom of God takes place. So that the convinced sinner who comes to the light, who waits upon God, and waits for him, has the witness of the Spirit in his own heart to the truth of what he feels, and of what he seeks. The Spirit bears his witness to the reality of his wants; to the deep sense that he has of his sins; to the honesty and integrity of his soul; to his fervent cries and earnest searches; to his real grief on account of his sins, and his earnest desire of deliverance from them.

Nor can such a soul look either God or conscience in the face, and say, I am neither awakened nor quickened; I am neither in earnest, honest, nor sincere. Nor dare he say, I have no hunger nor thirst after God, nor that I neither labour nor am heavy laden. Nor dare he say that he has neither hope nor expectation of better days and better tidings; nor dare he say that there is no truth in him, nor that God has done nothing for him; nor would he change states, miserable as he is, with the most secure Pharisee, nor with the most gifted professor in the world; nor would he part with his dreadful feelings, the chastisements, the reproofs of God, the bitter sense he has of his sins, nor the intolerable burden of them, for all the treasures of Egypt, unless he could get rid of them the right way; namely, by an application of the atoning blood of Christ.

He can smell the stinking savour of a hypocrite in Zion, and feel the barrenness and emptiness of a minister of the letter; he can see through a sheep's skin on a wolf's back, and knows the empty sound of swelling words.

Neither the graceless heart of a foolish virgin, nor the arrogance of them that talk of liberty while they are the servants of corruption, are hid from him, though he is fast bound in affliction and iron. He is a strange creature both to himself and others. He speaks a language that few can understand; and it is a language which he himself cannot explain. He is always in action, and acts a part that astonishes himself. He sucks his sweets from bitterness, Prov. 27:7, and cleaves to the rod that beats him.

By affliction he lives, and in the shadow of death he finds the most life. He gets health in his sickness, and healing in his wounds; satisfaction in sorrow; life in death; faith in severity; hope in heaviness; and expectation in self-despair.

His burden is more than he can bear, yet he dreads the thought of losing it. He is completely miserable, yet he hates ease. And, though his life hangs in doubt, he trembles at the thoughts of security. And that which he is most afraid of, is that which he seeks most after. None work so hard as he, and none so great an enemy to works. To secure himself is all his concern, and yet he hates himself more than he hates the devil.

Beloved, farewell; be of good comfort, follow peace, and the God of truth and peace shall be with you. I add no more.

the twelfth meditation

XII

The Twelfth Meditation

AMBASSADORS personate their sovereigns, and are as their mouth in foreign courts; and are, or should be, respected according to their wisdom and faithfulness, and according to the greatness, dignity, and formidability of their royal masters.

But, O, what an honour is it to be an ambassador of the King of Kings! called and commissioned, owned and honoured, by him; and to be in a pardoned and justified state; in union, in fellowship, and at peace with him: and therefore ambassadors of peace, bearers of good tidings, publishers of salvation, that say unto Zion, 'Thy God reigneth!'

Such are the chariots of the Lord of hosts, in which he rides, and by which he bears his name among the Gentiles; out of which he shines, from whom he sends out his line into all the earth, and his words to the end of the world. Infinite condescension is this.

And when we consider what we were; how mean! how low! how poor! how despicable! But he hath chosen the poor, the weak, the foolish, and the base, that he may stain the pride of human glory, and bring into contempt the honourable of the earth. 'Now he which establisheth us with you in Christ, and hath anointed us, is God: who hath also sealed us, and given the earnest of the Spirit in our hearts', II Cor. 1:21,22. Upon this subject I shall now proceed.

The Holy Spirit is to aid and assist the true worshippers of God in every branch of religious worship; and the saints must serve in newness of spirit, and not in the oldness of the letter. God requires worship suitable to his nature; 'God is a spirit, and they that worship him must worship him in spirit and in truth.' Worship in the spirit is opposed to all carnal worship with a dead form, in which the body only is engaged; and therefore called bodily exercise, which profiteth little.

Worshipping God in truth is opposed to all false, deceitful, and hypocritical worship, when the heart and soul are altogether disengaged: 'They draw near to me with their mouth, and with their lips do honour me, but their heart is far from me; therefore in vain they worship me.'

In order to truly worship we must be purged and purified, justified and sanctified, and influenced with the Holy Spirit of God. God requires a pure offering, and an offering in righteousness, or offerings offered up by persons in a justified state. 'And he shall sit as a refiner and purifier of silver: and he shall purify the sons of Levi, and purge them as gold and silver, that they may offer unto the LORD an offering in righteousness. Then shall the offering of Judah and Jerusalem be pleasant unto the LORD, as in the days of old, and as in former years', Mal. 3:3,4.

The days of old, and the ancient times spoken of, are the days of Abel, Seth, Enoch, Noah, Abraham, Melchizedek, Isaac, Jacob, and his seed, of whom, and of whose worship, we hear no fault, for they obtained a good report through faith. Now God promises that, under the gospel, the same acceptable worship shall be performed; and therefore he promises to influence and guide us in every branch of it; 'For I the LORD love judgment, I hate robbery for burnt offering; and I will direct their work in truth, and I will make an everlasting covenant with them', Isaiah 61:8.

And the Lord directs us in all our works by his Holy Spirit, and especially in prayer: 'Likewise the Spirit also helpeth our infirmities; for we know not what we should pray for as we ought: but the Spirit itself maketh intercession for us with groanings which cannot be uttered. And he that searcheth the hearts knoweth what is the mind of the Spirit, because he maketh intercession for the saints according to the will of God', Rom. 8:26,27. The apostle here tells us that we know not what we should pray for as we ought, unless the Spirit helps us.

And there are prayers that have been put up by good men that have not been answered: 'Elijah requested for himself that he might die, and said, It is enough: now, O LORD, take away my life; for I am not better than my fathers', I Kings 19:4. Zebedee's wife's request for her two sons, to sit, one at the right hand of Christ, and the other at the left, meets with no better answer than this, 'Ye know not what ye ask', Matt. 20:22. Which shows us the need of a Spirit of grace and supplication.

The Holy Spirit enlightens us to see our wants, and quickens us to feel them, and creates a hunger and a thirst after the provision of God's house; and then leads our minds into the word, and shows us what is held forth, promised, and freely given to us; 'Now we have received, not the spirit of the world, but the spirit which is of God; that we might know the things that are freely given to us of God', I Cor. 2:12.

The Holy Spirit, which searcheth the deep things of God, knows what is in reserve for us, and the time appointed for us to receive that which God hath laid up for us; and he sets us to praying for them when that time arrives.

Thus, when the time of Israel's deliverance from Egyptian bondage drew near, the spirit of supplication was poured out, and the cries of the children of Israel went up. 'And God heard their groaning; and God remembered his covenant with Abraham, with Isaac, and with Jacob. And God looked upon the children of Israel, and God had respect unto them.' So, in Daniel, just as the time was approaching for them to return to their own land, Daniel understands, by the prophecies of Jeremiah, that God would accomplish seventy years in the desolations of Jerusalem; then Daniel sets his face to the Lord God, to seek by prayer and supplications, with fasting, and sackcloth, and ashes, Dan. 9:3.

So, also, there is a set time to favour Zion, and every one that is ordained to be of her community; a set time for every purpose; and, when that time is up, which the Holy Spirit is perfectly acquainted with, then he makes intercession with such energy, that the kingdom of heaven, which suffereth violence, is taken by force.

The Holy Spirit furnishes the soul with suitable promises to plead, with invitations and encouraging passages of scripture: these he brings to the mind and puts into the mouth, enabling the soul to use all sorts of arguments, pleadings, intercessions, supplications, confessions, and reasonings: and, at the same time, helps the poor creature against his unbelief, misgivings of heart, desponding thoughts, shame, fear, and confusion of face.

He draws forth faith into lively exercise, and raises up hopes and expectations of being heard and answered. He emboldens the poor sinner, and fortifies his mind; he strengthens his heart, silences his accusers, and clothes his words with power; enabling him to pour out his very soul before God with earnest cries and tears, till his cares and concerns, his burdens, his griefs, his distresses and sorrows, his doubts and fears, all flow out with his words; and he goes from Shiloh with his countenance no more sad.

How did he help Manasseh, who was an idolater and a wizard, who made Judah and Jerusalem do worse than the heathen, and who was deaf to all warning and admonition, till God brought an host against him, who took him and bound him with fetters, and carried him to Babylon? 'And when he was in affliction, he besought the LORD his God, and humbled himself greatly before the God of his fathers, and prayed unto him; and he was entreated of him, and heard his supplication, and brought him again to Jerusalem into his kingdom. Then Manasseh knew that the LORD he was God', II Chron. 33:12,13.

How did the Holy Spirit furnish the poor Syrophenician woman with her great faith and treble plea, till she got all her heart's desire? He made the poor prodigal claim his sonship in a far country, even when stung with the guilt of sinning against heaven and before God, as his own father in covenant. Hezekiah, also, when both heaven and earth seemed to combine against him.

Some of the children of God, who have foully fallen, and brought on themselves, and on God's cause and family, open reproach and scandal; as Noah, David, Peter; and others also who have awfully backslidden, and got into sin and into the world, till their hearts have been almost hardened from fear, and who would have gone from bad to worse, till they had become quite callous, and return no more, had not the Holy

Spirit, either by his own immediate operations, or by the instrumentality of some Nathan, alarmed and awakened them to a sense of their state.

And when they were awakened, and brought to a sense of their sins, their crimes were aggravated with such a complication of circumstances, and attended with such bitter reflections, as would have sunk them for ever, had not the power of the Spirit been put forth in them. Sins against light and love; against comfort, joy, and peace; against a merciful and compassionate Father; against all the blessings of the better testament; against a God formerly known and enjoyed, and against a Saviour revealed, and after union, communion and fellowship with him; and against the consolations, witnessing, and sealing of the Holy Spirit of promise. Sins against the memory of the glorious times that are past, the blessed days of the Son of man; and the joy, peace, rest, quietude, and happiness then enjoyed.

But now all is gone. 'Fool that I am', says the poor creature; 'for a little pelf, a little imagined pleasure; and now by the deceitfulness of sin, am I shorn of all my strength and divested of all true happiness. I have stumbled the weak, and have opened the mouths of the enemies of my God: they that have watched for my halting, and who would rejoice when I am moved, these who eat up God's people as they eat bread, will now say, This is the day that we have looked for. My smiling God is gone, and all sweet intercourse appears to be cut off.

'The Holy Spirit is grieved; no access to a throne of grace, no liberty in the Spirit, no freedom of speech. A dismal gloom appears in the bible, nothing but reproofs and rebukes from the pulpit, barrenness in the pew, a fallen countenance before the world; and not a thing but secret rage, envy, and jealousy in my heart, when I am among them that love God, which casts a damp upon all their holy fire. O my base ingratitude! 'Fools, because of their iniquities, are afflicted.' I may go halting to my grave under fatherly severity, and perhaps it will be worse than that. Who knows but I have committed the unpardonable sin, and have crucified Christ afresh, and done despite to the Spirit of grace, and therefore am a castaway?'

A sheep thus strayed would never return, a soul thus fallen would never rise more, without the assistance of the Holy Spirit. David knew this when he prayed, 'Cast me not away from thy presence; and take not thy Holy Spirit from me', Psalm 51:11.

A soul thus exercised watches, observes, and attends all the day long to the Holy Spirit, to see if he can find any enlargement of heart, any risings of hope and expectation, any goings forth in faith or affection, any freedom of soul or of speech in prayer, any flowings out of godly sorrow, any soundings of the bowels after God, any real compunction, contrition, or pious mourning after the Lord; if there be any goings forth of love to him; if any filial or childlike fear of him springing up, having the goodness of God for its object; if he can find any fortitude, help, or inward support, or assistance in prayer; if any word come to assuage his grief, to soften the heart, to support, encourage or to produce submission to the will of God; if there be any dispersion of his fears and terrors; if any self-abhorrence or self-loathing; if Satan's accusations and fiery darts lose their force, or abate in their violence; if the reproaches of conscience get less severe.

Thus does the poor distressed soul wait upon the Holy Spirit, and watch and observe every influence, operation, or change, that is made in the heart and greedily catches every hint, dictate, sensation, motion, affection, allurement, or encouragement, which is produced in the inward parts, and weighs it, considers it, embraces it, and interprets it in his own favour, as far as circumstances, truth, and conscience will permit him.

Sometimes souls under such relapses find that the law is armed with fresh wrath and terrors against them, and that bitter things in lawful handwriting appear against them; that this lays a fresh hold of them, and binds them fast: 'The strength of sin is the law', I Cor. 15:56. The spirit of bondage seizes them and shuts them up; which is nothing else but the anger of God working wrath, slavish fear, terror, and torment in them; under which they are contracted, bound, and hemmed in; shut up in unbelief, in hardness of heart, and under the rebukes of God, and in fear of worse to come; and while thus imprisoned neither faith nor love dare to venture out.

Hence David complains, 'Save me, O God, for the waters are come in unto my soul. I sink in deep mire, where there is no standing: I am come into deep waters, where the floods overflow me. I am weary of my crying: my throat is dried: mine eyes fail while I wait for my God', Ps. 69. 'Wash me throughly from mine iniquity, and cleanse me from my sin. For I acknowledge my transgressions: and my sin is ever before me. Purge me with hyssop, and I shall be clean: wash me, and I shall be whiter than snow. Restore unto me the joy of thy salvation; and uphold me with thy free spirit', Psalm 51.

And again, 'O my God, my soul is cast down within me: therefore will I remember thee from the land of Jordan, and of the Hermonites, from the hill Mizar. Deep calleth unto deep at the noise of thy waterspouts: all thy waves and thy billows are gone over me', Psalm 42.

In all this the psalmist feels the spirit of bondage, the sense of wrath and fear; and he prays for the joy of God's salvation, and to be upheld by God's free spirit; which is the Holy Spirit, the spirit of love and power. He complains of a certain deep calling unto deep.

A soul in the horrible pit hears little else but the calls of law and justice for vengeance, which are always answered again by the accusations of Satan in the conscience. The storms of Sinai, like a waterspout at sea, threaten the vessel with a deluge of wrath, which would soon drown it in destruction and perdition. The waves of displeasure, rolling over the poor creature, are ready to send the bark to the bottom. This is the terrible way in which some fallen and backsliding souls are purged and reclaimed; and especially such as have brought public scandal upon the gospel and church of Christ, as, for example, the incestuous person at Corinth.

Others are revived and restored by more gentle means; a soft tongue shall break their bones, Prov. 25:15; or divine kindness shall melt, humble and soften them. But even this unexpected kindness, which is coyly received, and in much self-abhorrence often put away, as if one were utterly unworthy of the least notice of God, is mixed with some resentment, which keeps the soul at a distance, joining fear with trembling.

This appears when the child of God is raised up and restored as the poor prodigal was: the kiss, the robe, and the ring, quite killed him; or when a propitious look from the Lord Jesus Christ killed Peter to sin, self, and the world, as he went out, and with a flood of tears of penitence and love, wept bitterly.

Such are forgiven; but it is long before they can forgive themselves. They are acquitted by God, but they will not suffer their conscience to acquit themselves. What carefulness it works in them! yea, what clearing of themselves! yea, what indignation! yea, what fear! yea, what vehement desire! yea, what zeal! yea, what revenge! II Cor. 7:11.

Thus the Holy Spirit helps the infirmities of the saints of God through the mediation of Jesus Christ; and continually communicates grace from his fulness to help them in every time of need; whose inexhaustible fulness of grace is sufficient to change the heart of the stoutest rebel, to raise up those fearfully fallen, and to restore the most awful backslider.

'Howbeit for this cause I obtained mercy, that in me first Jesus Christ might show forth all longsuffering, for a pattern to them which should hereafter believe on him to life everlasting. Now unto the King eternal, immortal, invisible, the only wise God, be honour and glory for ever and ever. Amen', I Tim. 1:16,17.

the thirteenth meditation

XIII

The Thirteenth Meditation

BELOVED, the perishing soul, parched under the heat of a fiery law, led to the fountain of living water, is to drink, and shall have a well of living water in his heart, which is to spring up into everlasting life.

I know that Christ has rent the heavens and come down; that there is a new and living way opened into the holy of holies; and that he has admitted our hearts and hopes, our faith and our affections, already to the right hand of God where he sitteth; and where our heart is, there is our treasure.

And there is nothing that men delight in more than their treasure: of this they boast, and on this they set their mind, and generally it employs their thoughts; and therefore you must not wonder if I come again and again to set down my meditations, for we have heavenly treasure even in earthen vessels, as it is written, II Cor. 4:7.

The next thing that I shall treat of is the assistance of the Holy Spirit against the work of Satan. 'So shall they fear the name of the LORD from the west, and his glory from the rising of the sun. When the enemy shall come in like a flood, the Spirit of the LORD shall lift up a standard against him. And the Redeemer shall come to Zion', Isa. 59:19,20.

Every time that a new-born soul experiences the hiding of God's countenance, or is put into the furnace of affliction, or is exercised with legal bondage or spiritual desertions, the adversary is sure to be upon him, to raise doubts and fears in him, by calling the whole work of God upon his soul into question; and, by raising scruples in his mind, he rouses up the unbelief of his heart; and then he deals with the poor soul just as a highwayman does with the unwary traveller; he comes upon him unexpectedly, and flurries him, and fills him with confusion, so that he is robbed before he can recollect himself.

So the believer, when his comforts are gone, is suddenly surprised by the various assaults of Satan; 'As the birds that are caught in the snare, so are the sons of men snared in an evil time, when it falleth suddenly upon them', Eccl. 9:12. The devil labours to dispute him out of the truth of the work of God in his heart, by setting before him such as the foolish virgins and how far they went on; the gifts and abilities of Judas, and what became of him; and of many in the present day, who made a great show and deceived many.

Moreover, Satan suggests to the young believer that the real children of God receive a Comforter that abides with them for ever, and therefore they are always comfortable; and that no such temptations befall the real saints of God, for, 'He that is begotten of God keepeth himself, and that wicked one toucheth him not', I John 5:18. 'The blood of Christ cleanseth (them) from all sin', and, 'Whosoever is born of God doth not commit sin', I John 3:9.

'Whereas', saith Satan, 'you are full of sin and hardness of heart, full of rebellion and unbelief, and all manner of concupiscence. No, no; do not deceive yourself', saith he, 'the saints of God are purged, and therefore clean; they are washed, and they are whiter than snow: whereas you are as black as the tents of Kedar, and are filled with secret rage and envy at those that do really love and fear God; and this is an infallible mark of an hypocrite: For they that hate Zion shall be desolate.'

'This', says Satan, 'was the case and state of Saul, king of Israel; he hated David because the Lord was with him. And this upon him was an evident token of perdition; for he that hateth his brother is as Cain, who was of that wicked one, and slew his brother; yea, he that hateth his brother is a murderer; and ye know that no murderer hath eternal life abiding in him.

'Besides, you really hate those that truly love God because they are happy, and because you see and know that the Lord is with them; this is hating the Holy Comforter also; and, if this be not doing despite to the Spirit of grace, what is?

'Moreover, real believers are kept by the mighty power of God through faith unto salvation; but where is your keeping? Have I not access to you when I please? Are you not at this time in my hands? You have often, and (as you thought) with the deepest self-abhorrence, confessed your own vileness, and told God that had he destroyed you he would have been strictly righteous, for you have been an awful sinner against him. God only softened your heart and gave you a little joy, like that of the wayside hearers, on purpose to draw those confessions out of your mouth, that he may take advantage of it, and condemn you out of your own mouth, as a wicked servant.

'And not only this, but you have called God himself your Father, as the Jews of old did, when the devil himself was their father; and you have called Jesus Christ your dear Lord and Master, when you know at this very time that I have full power over you.

'Never, no never, was there such a headstrong, daring, presumptuous, God-dishonouring wretch as you. You a saint? You look like one, don't you? No, no: do not deceive yourself; all your joys and hopes, and all your comforts, that you ran from house to house and chattered about, it all came from me. I can transform myself into the likeness of an angel of light; I can counterfeit all the joys and comforts of the Holy Spirit on purpose to deceive. The whole work in you was all my own, and I did it on purpose to entrap you. Back to my work you must come, for you are still my captive, and I will make you fetch up all your lost time; and this the scripture declares when it says, And the last state of that man is worse than the first.

'Deceiving and being deceived. I have deceived you and you have deceived others. You have been to your minister and told him a thousand lies, and have deceived him; for he thinks it is a work of grace. And you have been to old Honesty and told him your experience; you have been to Dame Simplicity and filled her head; and to Miss Lovetruth, and she thinks you are a wonder. Go, go, and undeceive them all; tell them what you really are; that you always were a forward, daring, bold, arrogant rebel; and that you have added this, your deceitful and hypocritical profession, to all the rest of your innumerable and complicated crimes.

'Never, never more open your mouth, nor drop one word to any soul living about religion; yea, if your heart be hot within you keep silence, even from good words; for you will be a reproach, a public scandal, a byword, and an offence; and, Woe be to that man through whom the offence cometh. You will tumble these poor weaklings that you have tried to encourage, by telling them your experience; these will faint and give all up: and you know what Christ says to them who offend one of these little ones that believe in him, Good had it been that thou hadst never been born: yea, better that a millstone were hanged about thy neck, and that thou wert drowned in the depths of the sea, than that thou shouldest offend one of these little ones.

'No soul that ever appeared upon the stage of time, no character that is drawn in the annals of God, ever appeared so desperate as yours. Cain was banished from his father's house; Esau's cries and tears, and his hatred to Jacob, sprung chiefly for a blessing in temporal things; and Saul's hatred to David was mostly because he viewed him as the rival of his family in a temporal kingdom: but your crimes are worse than theirs, put them all together. For you hate the people of God because the love of God is shed abroad in their hearts, and the comforts of the Holy Spirit are in their souls: and to be jealous, envious, and hateful, not only to the children of God, but even to the comforts of the Holy Spirit, is an evident token of perdition.

'Go, tell them all what you really are, and undeceive them; and tell them never to lift up either cry or prayer for you, 'There is a sin unto death, I do not say ye shall pray for it'. Tell them that all your faith was nothing but presumption, and that all your claims upon God were unwarrantable and daring intrusions; 'And the soul that doeth aught presumptuously, that soul shall be destroyed from among his people'.

'You will now be held up to contempt, and be made a public example to deter others; yea, 'A fugitive and a vagabond shalt thou be in the earth'. And, as for me, I will harass, worry, and drive you, as I did the mad Gadarene, into the wilderness. I never sweat nor tire. I will pursue you with unremitted violence, till I drive you mad and desperate.

'Law sinners, that know nothing of the will of God in the gospel, will be beaten with few stripes; the heathen, who are a law to themselves, will be beaten with fewer still. But you are an impostor, a hypocrite in Zion, and a sinner against the Holy Ghost; the hottest place in hell is your portion, and I will punish you, for I am the tormentor, worse than all the slaves I have, unless you will fall down and worship me.

'It is in vain to cry to God, for there is no God; nor is it of any use to plead the promises, for the bible is not true, I dictated it: it was compiled by cunning and designing men which I employed on purpose to deceive the simple. Hence many noblemen, and some of the most learned in all the nation, burlesque it and ridicule it as a mere fable and as an idle tale.'

Thus with violence doth the devil break in upon the young believer and harass him, when it pleases God to leave him for the trial of his faith, and that he may know what is in his heart; and thus he used to serve me. Well may the prophet say, The enemy comes in like a flood; for all seems to be swept and carried away before him. Nothing appears to be left but the bare remembrance of things past, and sometimes hardly that.

But, when the enemy comes in like a flood, the Spirit of the Lord shall lift up a standard against him. This standard is Christ Jesus. 'Behold, I will lift up mine hand to the Gentiles, and set up my standard to the people', Isa. 49:22. This standard is intended to gather together God's elect to Christ, as will appear in the following passage. 'Go through, go through the gates; prepare ye the way of the people; cast up, cast up the highway; gather out the stones; lift up a standard for the people. Behold, the LORD hath proclaimed unto the end of the world, Say ye to the daughter of Zion, Behold, thy salvation cometh; behold, his reward is with him, and his work before him', Isa. 62:10,11.

Christ is the rod from out of the stem of Jesse; he is the standard and the ensign staff; his everlasting love is the banner;

a daily cross and a crown of glory is the motto upon the banner; ministers of Christ are standard-bearers; these are commanded to go through the gates, to cast up the way, to gather out the stones, and to lift up the standard to the people.

But then we can only lift up the standard to the people, not in them. Whereas the enemy is said to get into them: 'When the enemy shall come in like a flood.' All indoor work belongs to the Holy Spirit. We can only preach to the outward ear, and set forth the Lord Jesus Christ before them, which is called lifting up a standard to them.

But it is the Holy Spirit that testifies of Christ to the heart, and that lifts up the standard against Satan in the soul. And this he does by dispersing all the darkness and confusion which the devil has spread over the mind; by subduing the inbred corruptions which the devil has stirred up; by enlightening the understanding afresh, presenting the Saviour as shining into the soul, and by drawing forth faith, hope, love, repentance, and godly sorrow, to go forth and flow out to him; and, at the same time, raising up and bringing forth to the believer's view the whole work of grace in his soul; by passing afresh the sentence of justification in the court of conscience, by brightening every evidence, bearing his own witness afresh, shedding abroad again God's love in the heart, and filling the soul with joy and peace in believing.

Now, says the soul, let my enemy come! No, no: Satan knows better; he will not face thee with all that armour about thee. He lays at the catch; he hates the believing voice of triumph. When he hears thee mourning alone and sitting solitary, then he will visit thee again with the words, 'Where is now thy God?' These are Satan's times, and he will let us know it.

But yet the Spirit lifts up the standard against him, and unfolds the banner of God's love, again and again, in the behalf of them that fear God, that his beloved may be delivered from the power of sin and Satan. 'Thou hast given a banner to them that fear thee, that it may be displayed because of the truth. Selah. That thy beloved may be delivered; save with thy right hand, and hear me', Psalm 60:4,5.

As sure as ever Satan obscures the blessed work, and raises doubts in the poor sinner's mind about the reality of it, so sure does the Spirit lift up the standard against him, and revives the work, and brings it forth again to the light, that we may behold the righteousness of God in it. God's Spirit does it over and over again, till he has strengthened, stablished, and settled us.

Our fruitfulness, also, is owed to the indwelling and operation of the Holy Spirit. 'But the fruit of the Spirit is love, joy, peace, longsuffering, gentleness, goodness, faith, meekness, temperance: against such there is no law', Gal. 5:22,23. Again, 'For the fruit of the Spirit is in all goodness and righteousness and truth', Eph. 5:9. Christ is our living root; the indwelling of the Holy Spirit makes us one with Christ; while the everlasting love of God the Father to us in him unites us to him.

From his fulness the Holy Spirit continually supplies us; 'And of his fulness have all we received, and grace for grace.' Present grace assures us of future grace; sanctifying grace in this life provides the pledge of glorifying grace in heaven. The Spirit takes of the things that are Christ's and shows them unto us; his undertaking, his finished work; his truths, doctrines, and promises, his righteousness, peace, and satisfaction; his mysteries, kingdom, and his power and majesty; his exaltation, mediation, intercession, and glorification in heaven above.

This is the work of the blessed Spirit; and this union with Christ Jesus the Holy Spirit keeps up; and, as we have life in Christ the root, the Holy Spirit communicates life every moment from the root to the branch; for our life is hid with Christ in God. And Christ says, 'Because I live, you shall live also.' Hence the promise, 'Their leaf shall be green, neither shall they cease from yielding fruit.'

And no small part of the saint's fruit is put forth in God's house of prayer, and by diligent attendance there: 'The LORD loveth the gates of Zion more than all the dwellings of Jacob.' 'The righteous shall flourish like the palm tree: he shall grow like a cedar in Lebanon. Those that be planted in the house of the LORD shall flourish in the courts of our God. They shall still bring forth fruit in old age; they shall be fat and flourishing: to show that the LORD is upright: he is my rock, and there is no unrighteousness in him', Psalm 92:12-15.

In God's house of prayer the united fruits of the lips are offered up, such as, honest confessions of sins, and humble acknowledgments of mercies received. Prayers, supplications, and intercessions, are offered up in the unity of faith and love. God is extolled by the high praises of Zion, by thank-offerings, and by blessings, and the celebrations of the perfections and attributes of his nature; such as his mercy, goodness, truth and holiness, love, pity and compassion, towards poor sinners in Christ Jesus. 'Let him that glorieth glory in this, that he understandeth and knoweth me, that I the LORD exercise lovingkindness, judgment, and righteousness, in the earth: for in these things I delight saith the LORD.'

Here the saints often have bowels of mercy drawn forth, and their hearts enlarged towards the poor of the flock, to relieve their wants; those that are enriched by Christ Jesus come not behind in this grace also.

Besides all these, there are internal fruits brought forth under the word of God, which word is said to bring forth fruit. 'We give thanks to God and the Father of our Lord Jesus Christ, praying always for you, since we heard of your faith in Christ Jesus, and of the love which ye have to all the saints, for the hope which is laid up for you in heaven, whereof ye heard before in the word of the truth of the gospel; which is come unto you, as it is in all the world; and bringeth forth fruit, as it doth also in you, since the day ye heard of it, and knew the grace of God in truth', Col. 1:3-6.

A word of reproof often produces self-loathing and self-abasement. A word of severity mixed with love produces humility and meekness. A word descriptive of the tried soul's case, attended with an increase of strength and encouragement, draws forth faith into lively act and exercise. A word of comfort draws forth love to God, and joy in him. A word that restores a backslider is attended with contrition and godly sorrow. A word that seals pardon to a fallen saint, fires his zeal, and arms him with indignation against both sin and self. A word of instruction that settles a doubting mind, or fixes a soul halting between two opinions, and which informs his judgment and discovers heresy and heretics, produces blessings and thanksgivings to the glory of God. A word that encourages and succours the tempted, excites love to Christ and hatred to Satan. A word that strengthens and refreshes the sincere seeker, produces patience, submission, and resignation to the will of God.

And, though these are sometimes short and transient, yet they are genuine fruits, and such fruits as are produced under the influence of the Holy Ghost, who applies the word, and works with it, and by it.

All these, and many more such fruits, do the hearts of God's children conceive by the word, and under the operation of the

Holy Spirit of God; which often fills their soul with pious grief, godly sorrow, or love to God, or self-loathing; so that they would be glad, could the discourse be stopped while they might retire into some lonely apartment to acknowledge his goodness, express their joys, or to pour out their souls before God; and are often grieved, when they go home, to find the blessed unction and the divine power abated, and the heavenly dew dried up.

There is a continual flowing of grace from the fountain to the holy city of Zion. The river of pleasure, that flows from the fountain of life, sends forth its streams, which make glad the city of God; and Zion continually plays all her springs back again in devotion, worship, and adoration: hence the church is called, 'A spring shut up, a fountain sealed.' Shut up and sealed under sore trials; opened and unsealed in times of deliverance: shut up and sealed to all rivals and strangers; opened and unsealed to the Lord and to his friends.

At times, when the believer is under sore conflicts, and the Spirit begins to sanctify the trial, the divine flowings are wonderful, especially in prayer; matter and manner, words and power, are so abundant, that the soul is as wine which hath no vent; he is ready to burst, like new bottles. He hath no sooner sent up the whole weight and sensations of his soul, but the heart conceives again, and he is constrained to speak, that he may be refreshed, Job 32:19,20. But still the spring rises, till he can attend to nothing else. 'For my love they are my adversaries: but I give myself unto prayer', Psalm 109:4.

At such times the Spirit of grace and supplication operates in a wonderful manner; the believer, under the Spirit's influence is more formidable than an army with banners; there is nothing in heaven, earth, or hell, that can stand against him, as may be seen in Hezekiah, Isaiah 38; and in Daniel, Daniel 9:21; the former of whom drove back the sun in his firmament, and the latter fetched down an angel from heaven.

So, on the other hand, when the Holy Spirit furnishes the soul for praises and thank-offerings at the time of conspicuous deliverances from sore trials, temptations, or spiritual desertions, the soul is so banquetted, and the unction is so abundant, that the heart must pour it out. 'Thou preparest a table before me in the presence of mine enemies: thou anointest my head with oil; my cup runneth over', Psalm 23:5.

While we are blessing God, he keeps blessing us; 'In blessing I will bless thee.' His love flows in, and we pour it out; the sacred flame burns, and the continual burnt-offering goes up. But the former and latter of these are upon our solemn feast days, and at the commencement of the years of jubilee; for in the general, things are not so.

Think on these things, and follow after charity, righteousness, peace, faith, meekness, patience, with all them that call upon God out of a pure heart.

the fourteenth meditation

XIV

The Fourteenth Meditation

BELOVED, when I had finished writing my last meditation I concluded that the cruse was nearly exhausted; but this morning early it sprang up again, and seemed to flow over with fresh oil; it anointed my eyes, so that I perceived the meaning of this observation, 'The yoke shall be destroyed because of the anointing.' I found it was so, and therefore I pursued the flowing with pleasure, finding the service to be perfect freedom. My horn was exalted like the horn of an unicorn, and I was anointed with fresh oil.

O, that this were more observed and attended! But the believer is too much like the worldly miser, he never knows what he is worth. I must now speak of the things which I have made touching the king, and his anointing; and I hope that this will demonstrate that my heart has been inditing a good matter.

Firstly, concerning the judgment of the Holy Spirit. In the justification of our souls the Holy Spirit brings near to us the righteousness that was wrought in Christ when he died, enlightening the sinner to see Christ as the end of the law, as he works faith in the heart to go forth and embrace him; hence we are said to be justified in the name of the Lord Jesus, and by the Spirit of our God, I Cor. 6:11.

The Holy Spirit, by the ministry of the apostles, first applied the words of reproof and rebuke to the chosen of Israel, the remnant according to the election of grace, arraigning and bringing in many guilty. These all humbly craved forgiveness, and obtained it, when that blessed Spirit, sent to take of the things that are Christ's and show them to his own for whom he died, pointed these poor condemned sinners to the atonement and satisfaction of Christ, to him as their righteousness and reconciliation with God by the blood of his cross. Upon their believing, he filled them with the flames of love and zeal; and, sanctifying them, set them apart, devoting them as vessels of honour, meet for the Master's use.

You have this work and these people described by the prophet; 'In that day shall the branch of the LORD be beautiful and glorious, and the fruit of the earth shall be excellent and comely for them that are escaped of Israel. And it shall come to pass, that he that is left in Zion, and he that remaineth in Jerusalem, shall be called holy, even every one that is written among the living in Jerusalem: when the Lord shall have washed away the filth of the daughters of Zion, and shall have purged the blood of Jerusalem from the midst thereof by the spirit of judgment, and by the spirit of burning', Isa. 4:2-4.

Where this work is done there is a court of equity and justice set up and established in the conscience of the believer, that he may no more call evil good, and good evil; nor put light for darkness, and darkness for light. The law is put into the heart, and written in the mind. That is, faith being inscribed in the mind, and the love of God filling the heart of those to whom divine righteousness has been accounted, is called, by the apostle, the righteousness of the law fulfilled in us, while we walk not after the flesh, but after the Spirit.

Now, to keep things in order in the heart and mind of all God's children, God sets up this court of equity and justice, that we may daily cite ourselves thereat; and, upon every arraignment, 'If our heart condemn us not, then have we confidence toward God.' Our daily happiness depends upon our attention to this; 'Herein do I exercise myself', says Paul, 'to have a conscience void of offence'; for blessed is the man that condemns not himself in the thing which he allows.

To this end God promises the Holy Spirit to guide and assist us in judgment: 'In that day shall the LORD of hosts be for a crown of glory, and for a diadem of beauty, unto the residue of his people, and for a spirit of judgment to him that sitteth in judgment, and for strength to them that turn the battle to the gate', Isa. 28:5,6.

Brethren, take notice of the personality of the Holy Spirit in this text from the prophet Isaiah. Observe the personal character, titles, and names ascribed to him, the train of divine perfections: The LORD of hosts; a crown of glory; a diadem of beauty; a spirit of judgment; and strength to them that turn the battle to the gate.

The apostle, reproving some of the saints at Corinth for their unbecoming behaviour at the Lord's table, tells them that, 'If we would judge ourselves, we should not be judged. But when we are judged we are chastened of the Lord, that we should not be condemned with the world', I Cor. 11:31,32.

Did the believer attend more to this when conscience reproaches or checks him, going immediately to God by confession and prayer, disallowing and disapproving what he has done, not suffering his sin to go either from mind or memory, but importuning, and imploring pardon and forgiveness, he would soon prevail, and save himself many a bitter cry and restless hour. The Corinthians omitted this, and therefore God took it in hand. 'For this cause many are weak and sickly among you, and many sleep.'

David also neglected this, his soul hardening through the deceitfulness of sin, till Nathan set him where he ought to have set himself; namely, on the judgment seat. The prophet, by his wise parable, made David to condemn himself. But this, in his own conscience, by the Spirit, is what David ought to have done before. So it is that God judged and chastened, one way or another, so that his chosen might not be condemned with the world.

God not only keeps his court in the believer's heart, over which the spirit of judgment presides, but his house of correction abides there also. God purges the daughter of Zion and Jerusalem by the spirit of judgment and by the spirit of burning, for he keeps his fire in Zion, and his furnace in Jerusalem, Isa. 31:9. All those whom God judges he chastens; and this fire and furnace are to purge away their dross and their tin.

Many a time have I escaped that terrible furnace, by judging and condemning myself. And, though sometimes the process has continued for several days, yet I have followed it up, and could not, would not rest, till pardon was obtained, conscience quieted, and peace restored. Sometimes this has been done even in the pulpit; there the word has come and healed me.

Whereas some are in the furnace almost all the year round; but the reason is that they hardly ever make straight paths for their feet: that which is lame is turned out of the way instead of being healed, Heb. 12:13. Yet 'From all your filthiness, and from all your idols', says God, 'will I cleanse you.' This he does at conversion. But dross and tin still remain, and the furnace is prepared for the purging; 'I will purely purge away thy dross, and take away all thy tin', Isa. 1:25.

The spirit of judgment, and the furnace of affliction, are continually at work in Zion. Cold and lifeless frames; ingratitude for mercies received; yielding to unbelief and listening to Satan; murmuring and rebelling at the daily cross; deadness in the service of God; being often self-willed and soon angry; speaking hastily and unadvisedly with our lips; indulging evil and unclean thoughts; being stubborn and sullen under the rod; together with many slips and falls into sin.

Hence the complaints, 'Nevertheless, I have somewhat against thee, because thou hast left thy first love'; 'thou hast a name that thou livest, but art dead.' 'My people are bent to backsliding from me.' 'Hezekiah rendered not again according to the benefit done unto him.'Notwithstanding afterwards Hezekiah humbled himself for the pride of his heart. Hezekiah judged and humbled himself, and so escaped the furnace: 'Hezekiah humbled himself for the pride of his heart, both he and the inhabitants of Jerusalem, so that the wrath of the LORD came not upon them in the days of Hezekiah', II Chron. 32:25,26.

'If we would judge ourselves we should not be judged.' Upon every sinful frame and miscarriage God calls us to the bar of equity: 'Come now, and let us reason together, saith the LORD: though your sins be as scarlet, they shall be as white as snow; though they be red like crimson, they shall be as wool', Isa. 1:18.

When these things are strictly attended to, solid joy and lasting consolation is established in the soul. 'For our rejoicing is this, the testimony of our conscience, that in simplicity and godly sincerity, not with fleshly wisdom, but by the grace of God, we have had our conversation in the world.' The testimony of conscience and the enjoyment of peace are inseparable; and by attending to these a man walks with God, 'He walked with me in peace and equity, and did turn many away from iniquity', Mal. 2:6.

Some indiscreet members of the Lord's household are like some men who are embarked in several branches of business, and, being often cast down in their own minds, fearing they are going backwards, omit taking stock, lest a right knowledge of their affairs should sink them lower. But God will bring all his children to book; and, if they shun the bar of equity, he will bring them to the bar of judgment, and put fresh wrath and terror into the law, and hold up that handwriting against them; 'Enter not into judgment with thy servant', says David. 'Thou writest bitter things against me', says Job.

If we will not judge ourselves, the Lord will judge us; and if we will not reason with him he will make us hear the rod, and who hath appointed it; and then the question is, 'Hast thou not procured these things to thyself?' Then into the furnace we go, kicking and plunging like a wild bull in a net, full of the fury and the rebuke of our God; and here he keeps us till we can say from the heart, 'Not my will, but thine be done.'

'I will bear the indignation of the Lord, because I have sinned against him, until he plead my cause, and execute judgment for me; he will bring me forth to the light, and I shall behold his righteousness', Micah 7:9. By these means is the iniquity of Jacob purged, and this is all the fruit, to take away sin. Faith gets a fresh discovery of the atonement of

Christ, and a fresh application of it by the Spirit. If this be not the case, we come out like a fool brayed in a mortar. If so, there is not a deliverance from the furnace, but it is intended to confound us, and to keep us in fear and suspense; doubting whether the furnace is not going to be heated hotter.

When God takes us in hand, and judges and chastens us, we are sure of this furnace. I will bring them through the fire, and will purify them as silver is purified, and try them as gold is tried; and make a man more precious than the golden wedge of Ophir, Isa. 13:12.

But my brethren will say, 'If all our dross and tin are to be taken away, how comes it to pass that so much still remains? For no furnace that I have yet been in has ever removed the inbeing of it from me.' No: if the vessels of mercy were thus perfectly purged, then there would be no more presence of indwelling sin. But the root that bears gall and wormwood still remaining, the furnace remains. I can find that the furnace purges me from my evil frames; but not from the inbeing of sin, which betrays me into these evil frames.

Self is daily to be denied; the war between the law of faith in the mind and that of sin in the members remains, and is sure to be, more or less, directly or indirectly, the daily cross that a child of God has to take up. On account of these things the spirit of judgment remains in Zion. To subdue sin, and to keep grace upon the throne of heart and conscience, is the cause of this fire and this furnace in Jerusalem.

Self-examination is to the believer the business of every day. Every bill that conscience files against us is intended to bring us to the bar; but, upon trial, that which is most disallowed, disapproved, bewailed, lamented over, and the greatest cause of grief, and which makes us groan for deliverance, is the awareness of the continuing existence of the law of sin in our members: 'It is no more I that do it, but sin that dwelleth in me.'

Yet, withal, we are complete in him; without fault before the throne; and clean every whit, notwithstanding all these things that give the saints such constant distress and affliction in their daily warfare.

And now, my dear brethren, in observing these things, 'Whatsoever things are true, whatsoever things are honest, whatsoever things are just, whatsoever things are pure, whatsoever things are of good report; if there be any virtue, and if there be any praise, think on these things.'

'Now the God of peace that brought again from the dead our Lord Jesus, that great shepherd of the sheep, through the blood of the everlasting covenant, make you perfect in every good work, to do his will, working in you that which is wellpleasing in his sight, through Jesus Christ; to whom be glory for ever and ever. Amen.'

the fifteenth meditation

XV

The Fifteenth Meditation

BELOVED, continuing on from the fourteenth meditation, in proper order, I must now consider the mortification of the deeds of the body by the Spirit. 'For, if ye live after the flesh, ye shall die; but, if ye through the Spirit do mortify the deeds of the body, ye shall live.'

There is a great deal of mortification among the superstitious papists, pharisees, and legal work-mongers; but it all stands for nothing, because it is not done through the Spirit. 'If any man have not the Spirit of Christ, he is none of his.' Besides, whipping, thumping the breast, walking barefooted, fasting in Lent, abstaining from animal food, and confining oneself to fish, are all human inventions; for that which goes into a man defiles him not. And fasting is left to our own option; the Son of man came eating and drinking. It is not the lawful use, but the abuse, of temporal mercies, which the scriptures condemn. Besides, forbidding to marry, and commanding to abstain from meats, are expressly called doctrines of devils, I Tim. 4:1.

This work of mortifying the deeds of the body is called by different names in scripture. Our Lord calls it self-denial: 'He that cometh after me let him deny himself, and take up his cross daily, and follow me.'

It is called putting off: 'Put off, concerning the former conversation, the old man.'

It is called crucifying: 'They that are Christ's have crucified the flesh with the affections and lusts.'

And it is called mortification: 'Mortify, therefore, your members which are upon the earth; fornication, uncleanness, inordinate affection, evil concupiscence, and covetousness, which is idolatry. Put off anger, wrath, malice, blasphemy, filthy communication out of your mouth; lie not one to another, seeing ye have put off the old man with his deeds', Col. 3. Here we have a description of the old man, and of his members, all formidable in appearance.

Now there can be no putting this old man off, but by putting the new man on. Without the law of God in the mind there can be no war against the law in the members, and of course no daily cross. Where there is a renewed self that follows Christ in the regeneration, there will be a denying sinful self that hinders us in the way. The Holy Spirit raises up a new man in us, and then helps us to mortify the old man, that the new man may keep the throne: 'Sin shall not have dominion over you, for ye are not under the law, but under grace.'

Every attempt to mortify sin without the Spirit and grace of God, is as impossible as the Ethiopian changing his skin, or the leopard his spots. Satan is not divided against himself. No superstitious modes of mortification, which are invented by Satan, will ever hurt his reign, or destroy his kingdom. Whipping may wound the back, going barefoot may cripple the feet, and thumping the breast may make it sore. This is not merely neglecting the body, Col. 2:23, but actually abusing it. And for it all, the old man is still untouched, and of course unhurt.

Such mortification is wickedness; for no man should hate his own flesh, but nourish and cherish it, Eph. 5:29. The body is the workmanship of God, but sin is not. The body was very good till man let sin into it. The papists, legalists, and fleshly workers punish the poor body, but show lenity to the old man; these tender mercies of the wicked are cruel. Not the body, therefore, but the deeds of the body, the corruptions of our heart, are to be mortified through the Spirit.

1. The Spirit assists us in this work by testifying of Christ to the soul. Every time that faith is favoured with a fresh view of Christ, all grace is in exercise; faith looks and rejoices; love delights in the blessed object; hope abounds at the thoughts of future enjoyment; patience brings up the rear, in waiting for the change to come; humility and meekness sink the soul into less than nothing at the thoughts of a rebel being made heir to the inheritance of the saints in light. 'Put off concerning the former conversation the old man, which is corrupt according to the deceitful lusts, and put on the new man, which after God is created in righteousness and true holiness', Eph. 4:22,24.

2. By the Spirit helping our infirmities in prayer, God promises to subdue our iniquities; 'He will turn again; he will have compassion upon us; he will subdue our iniquities; and thou wilt cast all their sins into the depths of the sea', Micah 7:19. In this way the Spirit helped Jabez. 'And Jabez called on the God of Israel, saying, Oh that thou wouldest bless me indeed, and enlarge my coast, and that thine hand might be with me, and that thou wouldest keep me from evil, that it may not grieve me! And God granted him that which he requested', I Chron. 4:10. In this way Paul prevailed against his thorn in the flesh, the messenger of Satan that was sent to buffet him.

3. The deeds of the body are mortified by our attending to, and delighting our souls in, the influences and operations of

the Holy Spirit. When we follow after righteousness, peace, charity, meekness, patience, and faith, setting our minds upon them, and delighting our souls in these things, the old man gets neglected, and withers. 'This I say then, Walk in the Spirit, and ye shall not fulfil the lusts of the flesh', Gal. 5:16.

4. By leading us to love and to delight ourselves in reading and meditating on the word of God. 'Blessed is the man that walketh not in the counsel of the ungodly, nor standeth in the way of sinners, nor sitteth in the seat of the scornful. But his delight is in the law of the LORD; and in his law doth he meditate day and night. And he shall be like a tree planted by the rivers of water, that bringeth forth his fruit in his season; his leaf also shall not wither; and whatsoever he doeth shall prosper', Psalm 1:1-3. Here we are informed that this delightful work is intended to keep our leaf green, and to make us fruitful, like a tree that brings forth its fruit in due season.

5. The Spirit assists us in mortifying the deeds of the body by his quickening influences upon us, which keep up a keen appetite for spiritual food. Such souls thirst for the living God, and long for the courts of the Lord's house; saying, 'When shall I come and appear before God?' And such have their promise; 'Those that be planted in the house of the LORD shall flourish in the courts of our God: they shall be fat and flourishing; they shall bring forth fruit in old age, to show that the LORD is upright.' A keen appetite and a heavenly banquet employ all the powers of the soul: 'I sat down under his shadow with great delight, and his fruit was sweet to my taste.' And, when Christ's fruits are so sweet and delightful to our taste, the devil cannot vend his wares; the old man, with his deceitful lusts, are rather despised and blown upon than relished.

Moreover sorrowful meat is set before us in its season when the better sort is withheld, when there is a famine and a compulsive fast. 'Can ye make the children of the bridechamber fast, while the bridegroom is with them? But the days will come, when the bridegroom shall be taken away from them, and then shall they fast in those days', Luke 5:34,35. When these mournful days come, which are but too often, then Satan shows us all the kingdoms of this world, and the glory of them, and the imaginary happiness of his children, who war after the flesh. These are the days for sour grout, and for filling the belly with the east wind. But Satan never tells us who is to pay the reckoning, nor informs us about an eternal fast, and begging water in hell, when the Lamb and his wife will be bathing in endless pleasures in heaven.

6. The Spirit helps us in mortifying the deeds of the body, by exciting us to follow hard after Christ, and by encouraging us to cleave to him with full purpose of heart; to labour hard in order to our abiding sensibly in him. He draws us to remain in his favour, in the light of his countenance, in his peace, in his love; in the joy of the Lord, and in communion and fellowship with him; and all this by our constant visits to him, and continuing to abound in his work. 'I am the vine, ye are the branches: He that abideth in me, and I in him, the same bringeth forth much fruit: for without me ye can do nothing. If a man abide not in me, he is cast forth as a branch, and is withered; and men gather them, and cast them into the fire, and they are burned', John 15:5,6.

Here is the most sure way to abound in fruitfulness; the more we commune with the Saviour, the more we savour of his grace, and the more we are equipped against Satan and his wiles. Yet, on the other hand, if this be neglected and not attended to, we get at a distance, till sin, guilt, fear, and shame, stop up the intercourse, and then deadness and barrenness follow. Leanness comes into the soul, the heart sinks, the countenance falls; spiritual gifts, abilities, zeal, apparent liveliness, diligence, and all joys, seem to blight under the fire of inbred lust. Indeed, all wither away together, unless the Spirit displays his power again to draw the negligent soul.

7. The deeds of the body are not a little mortified by fiery trials. When the old man, with his deceitful lusts, is almost too much for the believer, in that even the faint and intermittent enjoyment of peace and comfort seem to fade away, nothing is sufficient to keep him. All is withdrawn; at this the soul is alarmed, anger lowers, fear and terrors flow in, and a spirit of heaviness succeeds. Doubts and fears about the goodness of one's state bring great concern; God seems to be gone; everything looks dismal; and the devil tempts the poor soul that he has neither part nor lot in the inheritance.

This in itself is a crucifying of the old man, with all his lusts and pleasures. This terrible remedy was applied to the incestuous Corinthian; 'In the name of our Lord Jesus Christ, when ye are gathered together, and my spirit, with the power of our Lord Jesus Christ, to deliver such an one unto Satan for the destruction of the flesh, that the spirit may be saved in the day of the Lord Jesus', I Cor. 5:4,5. Many times, but in a less degree, and not for public scandal, but to mortify the sins of the flesh, which are too strong for the believer in prosperity, the fiery trial comes on, yet it is only to subdue sin and purge away dross.

These, my dearly beloved brethren, are some of the kind helps with which the holy and blessed Spirit of God assists the believer in mortifying the deeds of the body. And eternal life will most surely attend and succeed this long and lingering toil and labour, which God has given to the sons of men to be exercised therein. Grace and peace be with all the brethren. Amen and Amen.

the sixteenth meditation

XVI

The Sixteenth Meditation

DEARLY beloved brethren: in this, the sixteenth meditation, I proceed to show the sealing of the Holy Spirit. This is promised to all that are taught of God, 'And many among them shall stumble, and fall, and be broken, and be snared, and be taken. Bind up the testimony, seal the law, among my disciples', Isa. 8:15,16.

But then what is the testimony? It is the gospel. And what is the gospel? The ministration of the Spirit. 'But if the ministration of death was glorious, How shall not the ministration of the Spirit be rather glorious?' II Cor. 3:7,8. He, therefore, that receives the Spirit and is born again of him, receives our Lord's testimony or witness; 'Except a man be born again he cannot see the kingdom of God. That which is born of the flesh is flesh; and that which is born of the Spirit is spirit. Marvel not that I said unto thee, Ye must be born again. Nicodemas answered and said unto him, How can these things be? Jesus answered, Verily, verily, I say unto thee, We speak that we do know, and testify that we have seen; and ye receive not our witness', John 3.

This doctrine Jesus spake; and adds, 'We speak that we do know'; and this he testified, 'We testify that we have seen, and ye receive not our witness.' This doctrine of the new birth, received in the experience of it, is emphatically called the testimony of Jesus. 'And I fell at his feet to worship him. And he said unto me, See thou do it not: I am thy fellow-servant, and of thy brethren that have the testimony of Jesus: worship God; for the testimony of Jesus is the spirit of prophecy', Rev. 19:10.

The testimony of Jesus is the spirit of prophecy. Hence it is plain that no man, in an unregenerate state, can be a prophet of the Lord nor a minister of Christ, nor a testifier, nor a true witness; for he is destitute of the testimony of Christ, which is the Spirit of prophecy.

Christ sends the Spirit into our hearts, and he is the living testimony and the witness; and we are witnesses of what he does in us through Christ. 'But when the Comforter is come, whom I will send unto you from the Father, even the Spirit of truth, which proceedeth from the Father, he shall testify of me. And ye also shall bear witness, because ye have been with me from the beginning', John 15:26,27. This is the testimony. The bond that binds the testimony is the bond of the covenant; and that bond is the everlasting love of God the Father, which is shed abroad in our hearts by the Holy Ghost given unto us, Rom. 5:5.

Thus God's covenant, in which he promises that the word of life and the Spirit of truth shall never depart from Christ nor from his seed, are received into the heart of God's elect, and are attended with the sweet blessing of God's eternal love to our souls.

'Seal the law among my disciples.' This law is not the moral law; for that was given by Moses, and which Christ came to fulfil: it is another law, that poor miserable sinners, who feel the plague of their heart, are commanded to wait for; for, as for the moral law, such sinners have got enough of that already, in their souls cursing and condemning them. But, to encourage them, they are commanded to wait for another. 'Hearken unto me, my people! and give ear unto me, O my nation! for a law shall proceed from me, and I will make my judgment to rest for a light of the people. My righteousness is near; my salvation is gone forth, and mine arms shall judge the people; the isles shall wait upon me, and on my arm shall they trust', Isa. 51:4,5.

This law that goes forth is attended with salvation and righteousness; but neither salvation from sin, nor righteousness to justify, are obtained by the works of the moral law. The Lord's arm is to judge the people. It is the arm of the Lord revealed that makes a man believe the gospel report; and he that believes is saved with this salvation; and the righteousness of God by faith of Jesus Christ is unto and upon all them that believe: they are justified; and that is their judgment which begins at the house of God first.

And this judgment of the people is to be a light to them in future; for every preacher, that contradicts or denies the justification of God's elect by faith, contradicts the gospel and the Spirit's work; therefore the Lord says, in the same chapter, 'To the law and to the testimony; if they speak not according to this word, it is because there is no light in them', Isa. 8:20.

Thus, my dear brethren, comes the arm of the Lord working faith. Salvation from sin, and justification from all things, attend believing. Such souls have taken their trial; their judgment is over; their cause is decided; and the decision is in their favour; they are pronounced just; and, of course, are passed from death to life, and shall not come into condemnation, John 5:24.

On this arm of the Lord are we to trust, and to say, In the Lord we have righteousness and strength, Isa. 45:24. And this our judgment is to be our future light, to try preachers and their doctrines by; these are to be brought to this law, and to the testimony that we have received; and, if they speak not according to this word, there is no light in them: and this is the judgment that we are to make of them. And how few preachers have we that can stand in this judgment, or in a congregation thus made righteous!

Upon believing we are to be sealed; 'Seal the law among my disciples.' This law is the law of faith; the seal of God never attends the preaching of any other law, 'This only would I learn of you, Received ye the Spirit by the works of the law, or by the hearing of faith?' Again, 'He therefore that ministereth the Spirit and worketh miracles among you, doth he it by the works of the law, or by the hearing of faith?' Gal. 3:2,5. Not by the law, for that worketh wrath, and all ministers of the law are dead men; we are not ministers of the letter, but of the Spirit; 'For the letter killeth, but the Spirit giveth life.'

The Holy Spirit of promise belongs to the new covenant, and he is the giver of the law of life; 'The law of the Spirit of life in Christ Jesus hath made me free from the law of sin and death', Rom. 8:2. Believers in the Son of God, whose hearts are purified, and whose souls are justified; these, and no other, are ministers of the Spirit. No other, however gifted, can convey the golden oil, for that always flows through golden pipes, Zech. 4:2,12.

Spiritual gifts, such as the gift of tongues, or that of working miracles, or that of prophecy, or that of understanding all mysteries, or of having all knowledge, or that of casting out devils, which is the best of all, are not the things that accompany salvation; men may have all these, and yet be nothing, I Cor. 13:1,2.

'Many will say to me in that day, Lord, Lord, have we not prophesied in thy name, and in thy name cast out devils, and done many wonderful works? And then will I profess unto them, I never knew you: depart from me, all ye that work iniquity.'

Balaam was a worker of iniquity when he prophesied, and so was Judas when he preached and wrought miracles; the love of money, the root of all evil, was in the heart of them both; nor did they ever love God, or seek his glory; they sought their own glory, and therefore they were not true men, nor was there any righteousness in them.

Spiritual gifts have their seat only in the judgment and in the understanding; and the word of God never goes any deeper than into their judgment and their mouth; there they hold the truth, and it is in unrighteousness, Rom. 1:18. The nobler faculties of the soul are never touched by these gifts, nor does the soul reap any benefit from them.

There is no divine power operating on the will, making them willing. He that God makes willing repents, and goes into the vineyard and does the will of his father. Nor is the conscience purged, nor the heart purified, by these things. There is no law written in the mind, nor any holy fire kindled in the affections, to raise them up to the right hand of God where Christ sitteth. If they have any confidence or peace, the former is only presumption, and the latter is kept up by the strong man armed, who remains in possession of his goods unmolested; and all their joys spring from the novelty of the doctrine, and from the operation of oratory on the natural passions.

Many of these gifts were bestowed on graceless men in the apostolic age, to raise reports, to send out a sound into the world, to excite curiosity, and to draw people to hear the word, and be witnesses of the power of God; which terminated in the salvation of God's elect, and which was for a witness against others, Mt. 24:14.

But, when the elect of God were collected together, and churches formed and endowed with the Holy Ghost, then the year of jubilee was come, and these gifts returned again to the Prince of peace, as was foretold by the prophet; and the men that were endowed with them either went into the world, or into all manner of heresies, and so became the pests and foes of Zion; just as we see some people do now. 'Thus saith the Lord God; If the prince give a gift to any of his sons, the inheritance thereof shall be his sons'; it shall be their possession by inheritance. But, if he give a gift of his inheritance to one of his servants, then it shall be his to the year of liberty; after it shall return to the prince; but his inheritance shall be his sons' for them', Ezek. 46:16,17.

Thus we see there is nothing secured to the servants when the year of jubilee comes; but the inheritance of the sons is richly secured. All which is punctually fulfilled by Christ; 'Take, therefore, the talent from him, and give it unto him which hath ten talents. For unto every one that hath shall be given, and he shall have abundance; but from him that hath not shall be taken away even that which he hath. And cast ye the unprofitable servant into outer darkness; there shall be weeping and gnashing of teeth', Mt. 25:28-30.

But God writes the law of faith in the mind, and the law of love in the fleshly tables of the heart; and where these come, there the year of jubilee is proclaimed, and the law of liberty is published in the soul; and, to make all things sure and secure here, God sets the broad seal of heaven to the work. 'In whom ye also trusted after that ye heard the word of truth, the gospel of your salvation: in whom also, after that ye believed, ye were sealed with that Holy Spirit of promise', Eph. 1:13.

Believers are living epistles, and as such they are sealed with an everlasting seal. Others may know these epistles and read them; but the choice contents, the mysteries, and the treasure, belong to God, and none else.

Seals are to keep things secret to the real proprietors, who can open them, read and delight themselves with the contents when they please, and seal them up again when they have done, and keep them close from all others: 'A garden enclosed is my sister, my spouse; a spring shut up, a fountain sealed', Song 4:12. The waters of this fountain are all sacred to the heavenly Bridegroom and his friends; when the Lord chooses that they should spring up in praise and thanksgiving to himself, or flow out to refresh his friends, they are opened, and will keep rising up and running over as long as this opening or enlargement lasts; and, when shut up and sealed, they always stop.

Sealing is to make things sure. So the Spirit seals the saints, that they may be sure that they belong to the elect of God. Assurance, therefore, attends the seal. 'Knowing, brethren beloved, your election of God. For our gospel came not unto you in word only, but also in power, and in the Holy Ghost, and in much assurance; as ye know what manner of men we were among you', I Thess. 1:4,5.

Assurance, therefore, is to the believer one of the blessed effects of this seal; as it is written, 'Until the Spirit be poured upon us from on high, and the wilderness be a fruitful field, and the fruitful field be counted for a forest. Then judgment shall dwell in the wilderness, and righteousness remain in the fruitful field. And the work of righteousness shall be peace; and the effect of righteousness, quietness and assurance for ever. And my people shall dwell in a peaceable habitation, and in sure dwellings, and in quiet resting places', Isa. 32:15-18.

The Jewish nation, called a fruitful field, was to be counted a forest; and the Gentile world, which formerly was called a wilderness, was to be turned into a fruitful field, under the out-pouring of the Spirit. Then judgment and righteousness were to remain in this field: peace, quietness, and assurance for ever, are to be the effects of judgment and righteousness.

Their habitation is to be a peaceable one: and so it is, for they dwell in the cleft of the rock, that is their habitation; 'Let the inhabitants of the rock sing; let them shout from the tops of the mountains', Isa. 42:11. They are to have sure dwellings; and so they have, for they abide in the Son and in the Father; 'Lord thou hast been our dwelling place in all generations', Ps. 90:1. And, 'He that dwelleth in the secret place of the most High shall abide under the shadow of the Almighty', Ps. 91:1.

They are to have peaceable resting places: they rest in the love of God, in the absolute choice of their persons, in his covenant, in the finished salvation of Christ, and in the Holy Spirit's work on their own souls; and I know of no resting places so precious and so quiet as these.

Paul calls circumcision a seal. 'And he received the sign of circumcision, a seal of the righteousness of the faith which he had, being yet uncircumcised', Rom. 4:11. Abraham believed God, and it was counted to him for righteousness before ever he was circumcised, that neither he nor his seed might ever glory in the flesh.

His circumcision is called no more than a sign of real circumcision; for a truly circumcised person is one whose heart God circumcises, that he may love him with all his heart, and with all his soul, that he may live, Deut. 30:6. Such, and only such, are truly circumcised; 'For we are the circumcision which worship God in the spirit, and rejoice in Christ Jesus, and have no confidence in the flesh', Phil. 3:3.

The real seal of true and spiritual circumcision is love; and circumcision in the flesh was a sign of this, and no more. This seal in Abraham's heart, and the sign of it in his flesh, was to assure Abraham that God would adopt, by national adoption, his natural seed, and give unto them the land of promise; which he did; and led them into it by the hand of Moses and Joshua.

And love was a seal to all Abraham's spiritual seed that he would adopt them by his grace, bless them with faith, righteousness and life; and that he would give them the heavenly country, and bring them into it by that renowned seed Christ Jesus, in whom all nations should be blessed.

Almost everything belonging to the believer is sealed; the foundation on which he builds is sealed. 'Hymeneus and Philetus, concerning the truth, have erred, saying that the resurrection is past already; and overthrow the faith of some. Nevertheless, the foundation of God standeth sure; having this seal, The Lord knoweth them that are his', II Tim. 2:18,19.

I do not understand this passage as some good men do; that seal here means the secret purpose of God, or his prescience. As to the foundation, the apostle undoubtedly means the Lord

Jesus Christ; as it is written, 'According to the grace of God which is given unto me, as a wise master-builder I have laid the foundation, and another buildeth thereon. But let every man take heed how be buildeth thereupon. For other foundation can no man lay than that is laid, which is Jesus Christ.' Now this foundation standeth sure; as the prophet Isaiah speaks, 'Thus saith the Lord God, Behold, I lay in Zion, for a foundation, a stone, a tried stone, a precious corner stone, a sure foundation: he that believeth shall not make haste', Isa. 28:16. From this text Paul takes it, and says, with the prophet, 'Nevertheless, the foundation of God standeth sure; having this seal, the Lord knoweth them that are his.'

Now this foundation, which is Christ Jesus, has got the seal of God upon it. 'Labour not for the meat which perisheth, but for that meat which endureth unto everlasting life, which the Son of man shall give unto you; for him hath God the Father sealed', John 6:27.

Christ was sealed with the Holy Spirit; he was distinguished, pointed out, authorised, anointed, and sent to be the promised and long looked-for Messiah. He was filled with the Holy Ghost from the womb, and sealed by the public descent of the Holy Spirit upon him at his baptism, just before he entered on his public ministry. The miracles that he wrought, and the souls that he converted, were all scriptural evidences of his being sealed and sent of God.

Hence the apostle concludes, that, though some, who confess the name of Christ, depart from the faith themselves, and overthrow the faith of others; yet the true Messiah, who is the omniscient God, and who, as man, is sealed with the Holy Ghost, must know who his own elect are; he must know whose sins he bore, for whom he died, and who are his own purchased possession: and surely he will never lose what his Father has given him, nor suffer any of those to be plucked out of his hand who are made his charge. The good Shepherd may suffer Satan to steal away the wolves, but not the sheep; for the Lord, but none else, knoweth them that are his.

Hence it appears that the believer's foundation is sealed, and so is the believer himself; and his sealing is said to be in Christ: 'In whom, after that ye believed, ye were sealed', Eph. 1:13. And thus God seals both the Saviour and the saved. 'Now he which stablisheth us with you in Christ and hath anointed us, is God: who hath also sealed us', II Cor. 1:21. Those, therefore, that are joined to the Lord are one spirit, for the seal of God is upon them both.

The choice treasures of the covenant also, or the spiritual blessings of the new testament, are all concealed and hid, under the same seal, from the eyes of all living; nor can any man ever get at them until the Spirit that seals the believer unseals the gospel, and leads the believing mind into it. 'The natural man receiveth not the things of the Spirit of God; nor can he know them, because they are spiritually discerned', I Cor. 2:14. 'And the vision of all is become unto you as a book that is sealed, which men deliver to one that is learned, saying, Read this, I pray thee; and he saith, I cannot, for it is sealed. Therefore, says God, I will proceed to do a marvellous work, and a wonder among this people: for the wisdom of their wise men shall perish, and the understanding of their prudent men shall be hid.'

And this came to pass in the days of Christ; 'Father, I thank thee, Lord of heaven and earth, because thou hast hid these things from the wise and prudent, and hast revealed them to babes: even so, Father, for so it seemeth good in thy sight.'

How many times, even before I was but twelve months old from my second birth, have I seen men in a pulpit labouring in the dark to get into the treasure of an eminent text which lay hid under the seal, but all in vain.

The sweet sense of pardon, of peace, of joy unspeakable and full of glory; the melting flames under a sense of eternal love; the sweet soul-dissolving sensations enjoyed under the divine flowings of godly sorrow and evangelical repentance, which are drawn forth under the sounding of God's bowels towards us, and the repeated discoveries of his love to us in Christ Jesus.

The heavenly sense and divine glee that springs up by the Spirit, under the impressions that attend the divine presence being about our path and about our bed; the sweet rays of divinity that often appear in the word, lighting up the deep mysteries and leading the enlightened mind, by a glorious radiance, out of one mystery into another, establishing the soul in the glorious harmony that appears in the word when crooked things are made straight, rough places plain, and apparent discords are made to harmonize.

The delightful and soul-enriching thoughts of poor worms being indulged with access to God, and with boldness, freedom, and familiarity with him; and to hold communion and fellowship both with the Father and the Son; and, at the same time, to see the word of God tally with all the divine teaching, influences, and operations of the most Holy Spirit of God upon us; and to be sensibly under the divine smiles of heaven; to be acquainted with the private thoughts of God's heart, which are thoughts of good and not of evil, to give us an expected end!

How many transient visits! how many transforming views! what sympathy does the God of all grace discover to us in troubles! what succour does he afford! what support does the heart feel in a trying hour! how sensibly does he rend the heavens and come down to our relief! Isa. 64:1. He admits our hopes within the veil, and our affections to his own right hand, where Christ sitteth. His blessed presence, when he shines upon the soul, casts a divine lustre upon the whole work of his hand; his brilliant perfections shine throughout; his glory covers the heavens, and the earth is full of his praise, Hab. 3:3.

The astonishing condescension of God, in stooping so low to visit us, makes us less than nothing. The distance and disproportion between God and such worms appear to be more, if possible, than infinite; and yet charity, that believeth all things, says, at the same time, and that with the witness on earth and the record of heaven, 'I dwell in God, and God dwells in me.'

The divine hints dropped for faith to catch, the mysterious leadings of his providence, the goodness that passes daily before us, and the mercy and truth that follow us; the watchful eye of God upon us; the most minute circumstances which are so sensibly observed by him; the deaf ear that he turns to all our exclamations against ourselves; the divine approbation; the love, the paternal embraces, which are forced upon us, which we, when self-abased, coyly shun and try to put away, judging ourselves unworthy his clemency!

These things, and thousands more, which my poor soul has enjoyed, and with which the word of God abounds, are all couched under the seal; which no natural man, however bright his parts, or however profound his learning, can touch, much less discover and bring to the light.

Natural men in the ministry are broken cisterns, wells without water, clouds without rain, lamps without oil, and a cruse without salt. One dead discourse from a minister of the letter is sufficient to cast the most lively soul into a deep sleep, to lay the most enlarged saint in irons, and to make a watered garden like a barren heath. Spiritual lethargy, legal bondage, and soul-beggary, are all that ever I got from such ministers; and I have formerly had enough of this hard fare. They turn a house of prayer into a prison, and freeborn citizens into slaves.

The believer, as a living epistle, has all the contents of God's laws written upon his heart, sealed and kept secret from the world; for the men of the world can neither see them nor believe them, though he declares them. He is sealed with the assurance of faith, which fixed his heart. He is sealed with the love of God in Christ Jesus, which is his circumcision, and a sure sign and seal of the righteousness of faith being his; for love casteth out fear, and believeth all things. Christ, his foundation, is sealed; the covenant, and all its rich contents, which are hid from the world, are sealed also and made sure to him; although neither concealed nor hidden from his spiritual sight.

Every wholesome truth, promise, or doctrine of Christ; every reproof or rebuke that gives instruction; together with all the cautions, warnings, and secret counsels, which are given by the great Prophet of the church; are clothed with power, impressed upon the soul, and fixed, as with a seal, upon his heart. 'For God speaketh once, yea twice, yet man perceiveth it not. In a dream, in a vision of the night, when deep sleep falleth upon men, in slumberings upon the bed; then he openeth the ears of men, and sealeth their instruction; that he may withdraw man from his purpose, and hide pride from man', Job 33:14-17.

Without this sealing Satan and his heretics would soon steal away the word sown in the heart; as we often see in men of the greatest abilities, when the word is only received in the understanding and in the judgment. These are often seduced and led to believe the greatest absurdities; and so would the elect themselves, were it not for the seal which attends the word. Truth, when sealed, makes the conscience free; and such souls set to their seal that God is true.

Truth, then, reaches the affections; it is received in the love of it. It is the word of healing that makes us whole; the word of faith which makes us believe; the word of power which makes us obey; the word of wisdom which makes us wise unto salvation; the word of health which cures all our spiritual diseases, attended with the abundance of peace; a word of light to guide our feet into the way of peace. It is the word of righteousness which makes us just; and the word of reconciliation which makes us friends. It is the promise of adoption which makes us sons; the promise of life which makes us heirs; and the promise of victory through grace which makes us more than conquerors.

All this, and much more, attends the sealing of our instruction. Hence the impossibility of the elect being finally deceived. Satan tries hard at the young believer, and sends the most wise and subtle servants in all his interest to do the same. But the young believer, just verged out of his bondage, and delighting himself in his liberty, and living upon little else but his divine comforts; and finding that these heretics bring nothing to his mind but confusion and bondage, which strip him of his sweet morsels, soon begins to be afraid of them; he shuns them, and suspects them to be thieves and robbers; and he is quite right, for they are nothing else.

And the Holy Spirit continues to revive and renew the work; this brings the soul again and again forth to the light. And every time the Lord shines into his heart the imposter is more and more discovered; while the young believer feels his own heart the more strengthened, grounded, and settled in the truth.

By this seal the image of God is impressed; and this is done upon the soul by the Spirit, while Jesus Christ is exhibited to the enlightened understanding, and to the eye of faith; as it is written, 'But we all, with open face, beholding as in a glass the glory of the Lord, are changed into the same image from glory to glory, even as by the Spirit of the Lord', II Cor. 3:18.

Various are the views that believers have of Christ Jesus while the Holy Spirit operates and makes this change, or impresses this image on the soul. Abraham, Isaac, and Jacob, Moses, Joshua, Gideon, and Manoah, all saw him; for he appeared to each of these, and many more.

Some saw him as an angel of the Lord, very terrible. Some in a human form, as Joshua; and in the clouds, as Job. Some as a flame of fire, as Moses. Some in suffering circumstances, as Isaiah. Others in his priestly habit, as Ezekiel and Daniel. Others in a war appearance, with garments dipped in blood, and upon a red horse, as John and Zechariah. Sometimes as the Ancient of days and venerable Judge, with his hair like the pure wool. Some upon his judgment seat, as Daniel. And others upon his glorious throne, as King of Zion, and above the cherubims, as Ezekiel.

O most precious, most wonderful and soul-transforming view! Others see him in the supernatural light shed upon the word. The word is attended with light and life. The Spirit testifies of Christ to the soul; at which time the Sun of righteousness arises with healing in his wings; which vision is promised to all them that fear his name, Mal. 4:2; and it is a promise of gospel times.

And this is attended with joy unspeakable and full of glory. 'Arise, shine, for thy light is come, and the glory of the Lord is risen upon thee. And the Gentiles shall come to thy light, and kings to the brightness of thy rising', Isa. 60:1,3. Which promise will be fulfilled, and found to be true, as long as there is a chosen vessel among the Gentiles to be called.

And, although we have many preachers who deny all vision, and of course all supernatural light, yet we know that such cannot be burning and shining lights, because they deny the light; nor ministers of Christ; for he makes his ministers a flaming fire, Psalm 104:4. Nor are they children of light, nor of the day; but of the night and of darkness; for, if what they assert be true, there is nothing but damnation in all the country: for God says, 'Where there is no vision, the people perish', Prov. 29:18.

Such blind guides have nothing to guide them but the light of nature, 'They speak a vision of their own heart', Jer. 23:16. To deny all vision is to deny God, who is light, and all knowledge of him. God promises that all his children shall know him; but how? God gives us the light of the knowledge of the glory of himself in the face of Jesus. It is to deny all the sure word of prophecy; for this is a light shining in a dark place.

Such deny the title of the saints, and all the good work within; for they are called the children of light and children of the day. They deny the path of the just, which shines more and more. They deny the salvation of God; for that is a lamp that burneth. They deny the lamp and the oil of the wise virgins; yea, and of the foolish too; for how could their lamps go out if they had no sort of light? They deny all joy to the righteous; for, 'The light of the righteous rejoiceth.'

Such men deny the scriptures of truth; for they are a light to our feet, and a lamp to our path. They deny all preaching the gospel; for that is sowing light for the righteous, and gladness for the upright in heart. They deny the being of God in his church; for, 'Out of Zion, the perfection of beauty, God hath shined.'

They strip a real servant of God of every name God gives him. How can he be a seer, a prophet, or a watchman, if he be stone blind? How can he be a burning or a shining light, a flame of fire, a candle on a candlestick, or a star in the Lord's right hand, if there be no light in him? They must be blind watchmen and dumb dogs; for what dogs will bark unless they see a stranger, or hear a noise?

And just such blind watchmen are all preachers who deny vision; for all supernatural light, which is above and beyond the light of nature, is vision; whether it shine into the heart, as in Paul, or into the head, as in Balaam; whether it shine in the word of God, or in the face of Jesus Christ. Paul calls this the heavenly vision.

Such men deny the dexterity of Satan; for Paul says that he is transformed into an angel of light. Yea, more; such preachers even deny their own deception, and the influence that they are under; for Paul tells us, that even imposters, or ministers of Satan, are transformed as the ministers of righteousness, II Cor. 11:14,15. In this account Satan aims to imitate an angel by his shining, and his servants to imitate the ministers of Christ by walking in the light of their own fire, and in the sparks that they have kindled.

The image of God, which the Spirit impresseth on the soul when it is sealed, stands in light, knowledge, glory, love, righteousness, and true holiness. And such souls shine as lights in the world, for they are converted; and real conversion is turning men from darkness to light, and from the power of Satan to God.

This sealing us is said to be unto the day of redemption. 'Grieve not the holy Spirit of God, whereby ye are sealed unto the day of redemption', Eph. 4:30. The day of redemption, here spoken of, appears to be the resurrection, which is the redemption of the body from the grave. As it is written, 'Ourselves also, which have the firstfruits of the Spirit, even we ourselves groan within ourselves, waiting for the adoption, to wit, the redemption, of our body', Rom. 8:23.

Now our sealing is the pledge and earnest of this. 'In whom also, after that ye believed, ye were sealed with the Holy Spirit of promise, which is the earnest of our inheritance until the redemption of the purchased possession.' In these words the church of God is called a possession, as it is the Lord's portion. 'The Lord's portion is his people; Jacob is the lot of his inheritance.' This portion is called the purchased possession, because it is bought with a price; 'Feed the church of God, which he hath purchased with his own blood', Acts 20:28.

The whole of this possession was given by the Father to Christ, and he laid down his life for it; and the price that he paid purchased the whole, body and soul: of all which he will lose nothing; no, not so much as a single hair; 'There shall not an hair of your head perish.' 'And this is the Father's will which hath sent me, that of all which he hath given me I should lose nothing, but should raise it up again at the last day. And this is the will of him that sent me, that every one which seeth the Son, and believeth on him, may have everlasting life; and I will raise him up at the last day', John 6:39,40.

This purchased possession is, at the present time, strangely scattered about. The spirits of just men made perfect are now in heaven. The bodies of thousands of the saints are now in the dust. Some part of the purchase now bears testimony; and some is in non-existence. But, at the resurrection, all must be collected together; all whose names are written in heaven, the whole church of the firstborn. And this will be the grand convocation, or the general assembly, Heb. 12:23.

Now the apostle tells us that we are sealed by the Holy Spirit unto this day of redemption; which shows that none but sealed persons will rise in the resurrection of the just. None but those that are of faith, and who, upon thus believing, are sealed with the Holy Spirit of promise, can rise in the first resurrection; for they, and only they, are blessed and holy persons. 'Blessed and holy is he that hath part in the first resurrection: on such the second death has no power', Rev. 20:6. Being of faith, they are blessed with faithful Abraham; and being sealed with the Holy Spirit, they are holy.

Hence this sealing us to the day of redemption is to assure us of a part and lot in this first resurrection; it is a pledge and an earnest of it. It is the Holy Spirit sanctifying and sealing of us that makes us meet to partake of it.

And this is a truth, that the Holy Ghost never will quicken and change any one mortal body, and fashion it like unto the glorious body of Christ, unless he dwell in it, and make it his temple in this life. 'Know ye not', saith the apostle, 'that your bodies are the temples of the Holy Ghost? Ye are the temple of the living God; as God hath said, I will dwell in them, and walk in them.'

This temple is holy; and, being blessed and holy, it must rise in the resurrection of the just; and truly blessed and holy shall it be when it rises. Christ raised up the temple of his own body; and the Holy Ghost will raise up the church, which is his temple, and fashion it like unto the glorious body of Christ. To these things, which are not seen, must we look. This, and what follows upon it, is the prize of the high calling of God in Christ Jesus. 'So run that ye may obtain.'

the seventeenth meditation

XVII

The Seventeenth Meditation

BELOVED, I think it meet, as long as I am in this tabernacle, to stir up your pure minds by way of remembrance, that after my decease these things may remain with you.

As to ministers, I say, meditate upon these things: give thyself wholly to them, that thy profiting may appear to all. 'Do the work of an evangelist: make full proof of thy ministry.' Bring the people off from their old sandy bottom, from all trust in the flesh, and from their sour lees of legal righteousness. Discharge truth in all its plain force and naked simplicity; and observe and watch its operations, its fruits and effects, and thou wilt find it sufficient, in the hand of the Spirit, to subdue the most stubborn, to change the most obdurate, to silence the gainsayer, and to furnish the man of God for every good word and work.

Next in my meditation I proceed to treat of the Holy Spirit as the earnest of our inheritance. 'For we that are in this tabernacle do groan, being burdened; not for that we would be unclothed, but clothed upon, that mortality might be swallowed up of life. Now he that hath wrought us for the selfsame thing is God, who also hath given unto us the earnest of the Spirit', II Cor. 5:4,5.

The apostle here calls our earthly bodies a tabernacle; which is a portable dwelling, set up, taken down, and removed, just as it pleaseth the owner so to do. This tabernacle, as it now stands, is not to continue, because of the misery which attends the inhabitants of it in its present state; we that are in it do groan, being burdened.

There is in it the plague of leprosy, and therefore it must be pulled down. There is a body of sin, a body of death in it; this has made it corruptible, and corruption is the seed of death: 'It is appointed unto men once to die'; God has made it subject to vanity, not willingly; for death, abstractedly considered, is not welcome to us; but God hath subjected it in hope. Death, disarmed of its sting, which is sin; and of the strength of sin, which is the law; and of the curse of the law, which is wrath and damnation; all which attend death as a penal evil: death, being disarmed of these, it is not death, nor the king of terrors; but the shadow of death, and the gate to life; for all things are ours, whether life, or death, or things present, or things to come, I Cor. 3:22.

The apostle calls these our earthly bodies clothes, which a man puts on in the morning. So we come into this world with this corruptible clothing; and, as a man puts off his clothes at night and goes to bed, so there is a night coming on for the Lord's servants, when they shall be paid; this is the time when those who have laboured under the cross, in faith and love, and in self-denial, shall put off their clothes, go to rest, and fall asleep in Jesus.

But this is not all that hope is conversant about. 'Not for that we would be unclothed, but clothed upon, that mortality might be swallowed up of life.' In that resurrection morning, when the marriage of the Lamb shall be consummated, this mortal body shall put on immortality and this corruptible shall put on incorruption. This is to be done when he who only hath immortality shall appear.

This will be the conclusion of the new creation, and shall be the last transformation for which we look: 'Looking for that blessed hope, and the glorious appearing of the great God and our Saviour Jesus Christ', Tit. 2:13. We have already put on the Lord Jesus Christ, and walk in him; namely, by putting on the robe of righteousness, the garments of salvation, and the covering of the Lord's Spirit. But in that day we shall put him on with a witness, and that for evermore.

The Holy Spirit will quicken our mortal bodies, and infuse divine life throughout every member of them, 'When Christ, who is our life, shall appear.' The Spirit will purge away, not only all our sin, which is called changing our vile bodies, Phil. 3:21; but will eradicate all corruptible matter, for incorruption shall be put on.

We shall then know in full that love of Christ which, in this state, passeth knowledge, and shall be filled with all the fulness of God, Eph. 3:19. The church is Christ's body, the fulness of him, all dwelling in him; and he will fill them all, be all fulness to them, and be all in them, Eph. 1:23.

Our bodies will not only be purged from all their gross and corruptible matter, which is now a clog and a weight, but they will be spiritual; 'There is a natural body, and there is a spiritual body.' This dead weight shall give place to an eternal weight of glory, II Cor. 4:17. It shall be raised in power; power to bear this eternal weight of glory, and power to bear the sight of seeing God the Father; for, 'The pure in heart shall see God', Mt. 5:8. 'In that day I shall show you plainly of the Father.'

In this power the body will be a fit companion for the soul; it will be vigorous, alert, and as the angels of God in heaven, Mt. 22:30. Hence, in the delightful service of God, there will be no fainting, no weariness, though we shall sing salvation to God and the Lamb for ever and ever, Rev. 5:13.

We shall be led by the Lamb to the fountain of living waters, Rev. 7:17; and, the soul and body both being spiritual, we shall drink of the river of God's pleasure, Psalm 36:8, which will fill us with divine fulness as fast as we can pour it forth in blessing, praise, and thanksgiving; together with the ascriptions of power, and riches, and wisdom, and strength, and honour, and glory, and blessing, to God and to the Lamb, Rev. 5:12.

Our bodies will be raised in glory. Our bodies, says Paul, are to be fashioned like unto his glorious body, Phil. 3:21. We, says John, shall be like him; we shall awake with his likeness. Divine light will shine in us with a radiance which will equal, if not exceed, the luminaries of heaven. 'Then shall the righteous shine forth as the sun in the kingdom of their Father. Who hath ears to hear, let him hear', Mt. 13:43.

At this time also, and at the consummation of the marriage of the Lamb, the spouse will be spiritually perfumed with all the powders of the merchant, Song 3:6.

The priests that attended in the holy place, near the holy of holies, were perfumed, Exodus 30:35,37; and shall this not be fulfilled spiritually in the holy of holies, eternal in the heavens, towards God and the Father in Christ? Sanctifying grace makes the church a bed of spices now, Song 6:2; then what will glorifying grace do? Prayers in the hearts of believers are golden vials full of odours, Rev. 5:8; but perfect praises in heaven must exceed them.

As perfumed with the sweet savour of Christ, God accepts us in his dear Son in this life; and in Christ we shall ever remain a sweet savour. 'I will accept you with your sweet savour, when I bring you out from the people, and gather you out of the countries', Ezek. 20:41. 'Awake and sing, ye that dwell in dust: for thy dew is as the dew of herbs, and the earth shall cast out the dead.'

All defects and deformity came into the world with and by sin; and, when this evil cause is removed, the disagreeable effects will cease; 'Every one that is perfect shall be as his master.' 'Christ loved the church and gave himself for it, that he might present it to himself a glorious church, not having spot, or wrinkle, or any such thing; but that it should be holy and without blemish', Eph. 5:27.

All superfluity, deformity, or deficiency, rendered a Levite under the law unfit for the priesthood, or service of the sanctuary; how much more glorious shall be the sons of God in the resurrection, praising without ceasing in the new Jerusalem? There will be no spot of sin, no wrinkle of old age, no scar of old wounds, not any such thing as deformity. Leah will appear without tender eyes, Jacob without halting, and Paul without the thorn in the flesh, and Timothy without his complaint. The church shall be perfect in one, John 17:23; and no imperfection shall stand before God. Christ was a Lamb without blemish and without spot, and we shall be like him, and see him as he is.

There will be a perfection of sight. The remains of the old veil hangs heavy upon us in this state; it is a darkness that is often felt; the dismal gloom upon the mind keeps us from looking to the end of things, and from viewing them as they really are: we see through a glass darkly, I Cor. 13:12, and only by the mirror of faith.

Faith is the sight of the heaven-born soul, which, like the moon, borrows all her light from the sun; for, if the Sun of righteousness shine not, if the Lord's countenance be not lifted up, we are walking in darkness, and have no light; we can only trust in the name of the Lord in the dark, and stay ourselves upon an absent God. 'With thee is the fountain of light: in thy light shall we see light', Psalm 36:9. 'For now we see through a glass, darkly; but then face to face: now I know in part; but then shall I know even as also I am known. For we know in part, and we prophesy in part. But, when that which is perfect is come, then that which is in part shall be done away.' 'Blessed are the pure in heart for they shall see God.'

And this sweet sight in the face of Jesus Christ is the ultimate end of hope, the fulness of expectation, and the superabounding banquet of all holy and heavenly desires, which shall fill them even to satiety. There we shall see face to face, and know as we are known.

There will be an end for ever to all grief and sorrow, and to all the causes of them. 'What are these which are arrayed in white robes? And whence came they? And I said unto him, Sir, thou knowest. And he said to me, These are they which came out of great tribulation, and have washed their robes, and made them white in the blood of the Lamb. Therefore are they before the throne of God, and serve him day and night in his temple: and he that sitteth on the throne shall dwell among them. They shall hunger no more, neither thirst any more; neither shall the sun light on them, nor any heat. For the Lamb which is in the midst of the throne shall feed them, and shall lead them unto living fountains of waters: and God shall wipe away all tears from their eyes', Rev. 7:13-17.

These are they which came out of great tribulation; from every sort of trial, trouble, temptation, and persecution, for this is the common lot of God's family. The robes washed and made white in the blood of the Lamb cover their glorified souls and bodies with divine righteousness. Their happiness is, that God dwells among them; that they are before his throne, and engage in his service, being filled with love to him and delight in him.

They hunger no more after righteousness, after life, nor after the word, being perfectly filled. They thirst no more after comfort, after the new wine of the kingdom, nor after the living God, being filled with all his fulness.

Neither shall the sun light on them, nor any heat. The sun of persecution and temptation, which comes because of the word, and which offends and withers so many unsound professors, shall smite them no more, nor any heat. Not the fiery darts of Satan, nor the fire of lust, nor a fiery law, nor the flames of spiritual and carnal jealousy, nor the wrath and rage of cruel men; for the Lamb in the midst of the throne shall feed them with his fulness of glory, and lead them to living fountains of waters; namely, to God the Father; saying, 'Behold I and the children which God hath given me', Heb. 2:13.

And God, Father, Son, and Spirit, are the living fountains of living waters; the fountain of life, love, joy, peace, goodness, glory, and majesty. And God shall wipe away all tears from their eyes, being presented unto the Father by Christ; and, being accepted, embraced, and blessed by him, all fear, sorrow, and grief, and the causes of them, shall be for ever banished, and of course all fears and tears about failing of his grace, coming short of the promised rest, and all dread about an eternal separation from him, shall be for ever wiped away. For, 'There shall be no more curse: but the throne of God and of the Lamb shall be in it; and his servants shall serve him: and they shall see his face; and his name shall be in their foreheads', Rev. 22:3,4.

These, my dearly beloved brethren, are some of the things which we have in view. 'Faith is the substance of things hoped for, and the evidence of things not seen.'

'Now he that hath wrought us for the selfsame thing is God, who also hath given unto us the earnest of the Spirit.' God hath loved us, chosen us in Christ, ordained us to life by him, adopted us, and predestinated us to sonship, and to heirship, and to the enjoyment of this inheritance; 'That he might make known the riches of his glory on the vessels of mercy, which he had afore prepared unto glory', Rom. 9:23.

He hath also reconciled us and redeemed us by Jesus Christ; he hath called us, quickened us, justified us, and sanctified us, regenerated and renewed us, tried and purged us; giving us faith, the substance of these things and the evidence of them, and begotten us to a lively hope and expectation of them. He has given to us the seal of secrecy, the seal of surety, the seal of ratification and confirmation; he has led us to subscribe to the seal with the hand of faith, which has felt them; and to set our hearty amen to these things, and our acquiescence with God in them, in which we believe and confess that God is true. And, to make things sure to all the seed, he hath given us the earnest of the Spirit.

This earnest of the Spirit is likewise called the firstfruits of the Spirit, Rom. 8:23. The end of the world is called the harvest, when the angels will reap the world and gather in the elect of God, and those who have sown to the Spirit in this life shall of the Spirit reap life everlasting. Glory in heaven is the great and grand harvest, when the master and Lord of the harvest will gird himself, and come forth and serve the reapers, Luke 12:37; when he that soweth and he that reapeth shall rejoice together, John 4:36.

Now, by the regenerating and sanctifying work of the Holy Spirit, the firstfruits of this blessed harvest are produced.

Christ is clearly seen by the enlightened understanding and by the eye of faith; and this is an earnest to us that we shall be like him, and see him as he is.

We see the light of the glory of God in the face of Jesus Christ; and this is an earnest to us, that all that are pure in heart shall see God.

Faith, which the Spirit produces, is the substance of things hoped for. To be found in Christ, and in the righteousness which is in him, is our hope, and faith is the substance of this; for Christ, the object of faith, dwells in the heart of all believers.

Faith is the evidence of things not seen; it is a clear and perfect proof both of our sonship and heirship. We are manifestly the children of God by faith in Christ Jesus; and, if sons, then heirs; heirs of God and joint heirs with Christ.

Faith is an undoubted certainty which silences all misgivings of heart. It is assurance itself, that persuades the mind, and stays it on the object believed in; it discovers future things to the believer, brings them near, and embraces them, and realizes them to the soul.

It believes in divine life, and applies it; it believes in atoning blood, and purifies the heart by it; it believes in an imputed righteousness, and puts it on; it believes in the promised comforts of the Spirit; and, 'We receive the promise of the Spirit through faith.'

It believes in the love of God, and receives it in the enjoyment of it, and works by it both to God and to his children. And what shall I more say? for time would fail me to tell the half of all that I have felt.

Heaven is a place of rest; and, 'We which have believed do enter into rest.'

Heaven is a place of peace; and, 'Being justified by faith, we have peace with God through our Lord Jesus Christ.'

With joy and rejoicing shall the church be brought to Christ, and shall enter into the king's palace; and God fills us now with joy and peace in believing.

Heaven is a place of endless day; and the path of a just man, who lives by faith, shines more and more till that perfect day be fulfilled.

The gift of God promised in heaven is eternal life; and, 'He that believeth hath everlasting life; and shall not come into condemnation.'

The inheritance above is endless glory; and even this begins in this life. 'Arise, shine; for thy light is come, and the glory of God is risen upon thee.' This fills the soul with joy unspeakable and full of glory.

All these, my beloved brethren, are the foretastes of eternal fulness, the streams of grace which make glad the city, flowing from the river of divine pleasure, the head of which is God, the fountain of life; for, 'Unto the place from whence the rivers come, thither they return again', Eccl. 1:7.

All these worketh the Holy Spirit of God through Christ the mediator, from whose fulness all grace is communicated to us, and through whom all grace flows back again, even to its own proper fountain.

What rich security is this, that the heirs of promise might have a strong consolation! God with his own finger writes his laws on the fleshy tables of our hearts, and puts them into our minds. He binds up the testimony in the bond of love to us; then he seals the law among his disciples with a comfortable assurance; yea, more, the Spirit himself is the seal. He is the divine impress of heaven, he stamps the divine image upon us, he affixes the truth and power of it, he makes and maintains a melting impression on the soul, he confirms and establishes the heart, he is the attestation and the ratification of all to us.

In his quickening, enlivening, enlarging, and cheering operations, he is the pledge of the first resurrection. In his operations of love, joy, light, and comfort, he is the firstfruits of the glorious harvest; and in all these the earnest of the future inheritance. Well may Paul say, 'It is of faith, that it might be by grace, to the end the promise might be sure to all the seed.'

Matters thus settled between Father, Son, and Spirit; revealed and made known, ratified and confirmed, by the triune God to his chosen and beloved family; testified by God's handwriting upon our hearts, sealed with the broad seal of heaven, and a pledge and earnest given: O this stands faster than mountains of brass; O the immutability of his counsel, the stability of his covenant, the security and safety of the blessed inheritance!

An earnest differs nothing from the whole lump in quality, only in quantity. The firstfruits are the same as all the rest of the harvest, only they are a very small part of an abundant crop: whether, therefore, we glean an handful like Ruth, or reap a sheaf like Joseph in his dream, it will at last terminate in a full barn. 'Gather the wheat into my barn', Mt. 13:30.

'O the depth of the riches both of the wisdom and knowledge of God; how unsearchable are his judgments, and his ways past finding out!' For of him, and through him, and to him, are all things; to whom be all glory, might, majesty, dominion, and power, both now and for ever.

the eighteenth meditation

XVIII

The Eighteenth Meditation

I NOW take notice of the different distributions and influences of the Holy Spirit. 'Now there are diversities of gifts, but the same Spirit. And there are differences of administrations, but the same Lord. And there are diversities of operations, but it is the same God which worketh all in all', I Cor. 12:4-6.

Now these gifts of the Spirit the holy apostle mentions. 'To one is given by the Spirit the word of wisdom; to another the word of knowledge by the same Spirit; to another faith by the same Spirit; to another the gifts of healing by the same Spirit; to another the working of miracles; to another prophecy; to another discerning of spirits; to another divers kinds of tongues; to another the interpretation of tongues.'

There is nothing in all these gifts that will infallibly assure or secure everlasting life in heaven to the recipients of them. 'The kingdom of God stands not in word'; neither in the word of wisdom, nor in the word of knowledge. We see many wise enough in the word that were never made wise unto salvation, who never had the knowledge of salvation by the forgiveness of their sins; and therefore, however wise they may be in the word, they are ignorant of their own hearts, and of the all-conquering grace of God in Christ Jesus.

Nor doth the word of knowledge, or the greatest gifts of knowledge in the word, secure the heavenly inheritance. 'Knowledge puffeth up.' Satan knows more of God, of the works of creation, of the efficacy of divine grace in sinners' hearts by his being so often cast out by it; yea, and of the scriptures of truth, the glories of heaven, and of the pains of hell; than all the natural men in the world, put them all together. Yet the weakest believer in all the church of God knows more than he. Men may have all knowledge, and understand all mysteries, and yet be nothing, I Cor. 13:2.

Nor is the gift of faith spoken of here that faith which purifies the heart and works by love; but miraculous faith, or the faith of miracles; which many have had to whose heart it never applied the atonement, nor put on an imputed righteousness; nor did it ever embrace the Son of God, much less bring him into the heart, and give him a dwelling-place there. It is like a faith upon sight, which many had, who, when they saw his miracles, believed. It is temporary, and for a time; those for a while believe, and then fall away.

This faith has its seat in the judgment and understanding, but not in the heart. It deals with the power of God in its operations, but not with the lovingkindness and tender mercy of God in Christ Jesus. And this power is put forth in working miracles on others, when it does nothing towards the salvation of the worker himself. And, as it deals not with the lovingkindness and tender mercy of God in Christ, it is nothing in the grand business of salvation; for, 'Though I have all faith, so that I could remove mountains, and have not charity, I am nothing', I Cor. 13:2.

Nor is there any salvation in the gifts of healing; such as healing the sick, the lame, the blind, the leper, or the lunatic, by casting out devils. 'Many will say to me in that day, Lord, Lord, have we not prophesied in thy name? and in thy name have cast out devils? and in thy name done many wonderful works? And then will I profess unto them, I never knew you: depart from me, ye that work iniquity', Mt. 7:22,23.

Nor is the gift of tongues, or the interpretation of them, one of the things which accompany salvation. This gift has its seat only in the understanding and judgment, and is played off from the tongue, but never reaches the heart nor the affections. Though some value themselves very much upon these things, yet no man will affirm that either Latin, Greek, or Hebrew, much less the language of heathen idolaters can purge the conscience of a guilty and filthy sinner. 'Though I speak with the tongues of men and of angels, and have not charity, I am become as sounding brass, or a tinkling cymbal.'

All these things have a tendency to lift men up; unless by the indwelling of the Holy Ghost, and by his humbling operations, they are counterbalanced, as they were in Paul and others. 'It is a good thing that the heart be established with grace', Heb. 13:9.

'There are differences of administrations, but the same Lord.' The Lord by the Spirit administers not only the different gifts to men, but grace; he administers strength to the weak in faith, increaseth it in them that have no might, making their strength equal to the day.

He administers the word to the preachers of it, and light to see into it; wisdom rightly to divide it; boldness to declare it faithfully, without fearing the face of any; zeal in the delivery of it, with lively frames to set off the sweetness and excellency of it, and power to enforce it; and that with the greatest confidence, from an inward testimony of interest in it.

And, without this divine influence of the Spirit, the preaching would be little better than a pillory, and the work of the ministry quite a slavery; as we see in too many who are obliged to have recourse to idle tales and old wives' fables, in order to fill up the time; or else to set up some supposed rival as a scare-bird, and call him an Antinomian, and so belabour him, just to help out; which is done for want of matter, and for want of the divine aid of the Holy Spirit. To these men I have contributed not a little, in thus helping them out at a dead lift.

By the Holy Spirit the Lord administers different power and authority to men; furnishing some to be apostles, some to be prophets, some evangelists, some teachers, and some to be helps; enabling each in his place to be of some use to the body, the church; that the whole, by the joints of one faith, and of one and the same judgment, and by the bands of love and peace, may be bound together; and that the whole, holding fast the Head, may have nourishment communicated from the Head, by the Spirit, to every part of the body: so knitting it together that it may increase in grace and in stature with the increase of God. See Col. 2:19.

Every one of these different gifts are of use in the body, when each, with diligence and affection, fills his place. 'For, as we have many members in one body, and all members have not the same office; so we, being many, are one body in Christ, and every one members one of another. Having then gifts differing according to the grace that is given to us, whether prophecy, let us prophesy according to the proportion of faith; or ministry, let us wait on our ministering; or he that teacheth, on teaching; or he that exhorteth, on exhortation; he that giveth, let him do it with simplicity; he that ruleth, with diligence; he that showeth mercy, with cheerfulness. Let love be without dissimulation. Abhor that which is evil, cleave to that which is good', Rom. 12:4-9.

Thus doth the Holy Spirit administer different gifts and abilities, and assign men different work in the church of God, to edify the body, and to keep it together, that there should be no schism in the body, no rending and dividing the affections of one member from another. And each of these is useful in his place; so that, 'The hand cannot say to the foot, I have no need of thee; nor the foot to the hand, I have no need of thee.' Now, as there are differences of administrations, but all these by the same Lord the Spirit, so, 'There are diversities of operations; but it is the same God which worketh all in all.'

The divine operations here spoken of are not those which are put forth in persons on whom miracles are wrought; for these, in the general, are only displays of divine power; but the operations of the Spirit in the souls of God's chosen are divers. And the infusing of grace into us, the forming the new man in us, the keeping and preserving us when formed, require divers operations. Though the new man, the whole work of grace, is produced at once, at the entrance of the Holy Spirit into the heart, yet it is not perceptible to us but by degrees.

The first thing that we discover of it is light; this was the first thing that appeared in the old creation; and so it is in the new. And even this entitles us to sonship, though we cannot by this alone claim it; such are children of light, and God is the Father of lights.

The next thing that is felt is life; and, when this quickening influence is spread through the soul, a mighty famine ensues; we cannot feed upon our former lusts and pleasures; these sweet morsels become bitter, and our former glory in the pleasures of sin becomes our shame. The famine increasing upon us, and former gratifications becoming nauseous, to work we go to get some entertainment or satisfaction from our own performances, and labour hard to fill our belly with these husks which the swine do eat; but the poor hungry soul can find no satisfaction in these.

However, there is now and then some strange emotion within, and some softening sensation felt; some distant tidings are brought to the mind by the sudden occurrence of different passages of scripture; and often transient beams of light, attended with a sense of soul-dissolving love; but their influences are so sudden, that they are almost gone before we can hardly relish them, which makes the appetite the keener.

But, when the Holy Spirit discovers Christ to us with all his finished work, and leads the soul forth in faith to embrace and console itself in his dying love, the new creature comes forth with all his beauty.

Then we are so taken up with the love and excellency of Christ, and with the unspeakable joys and consolations of the Holy Spirit, that we perceive but little of the new man; though this would be the time to observe him, when he is so lively, and the old man appears to be quite banished.

But nothing of this can be attended to till spiritual desertions make us doubt and fear; and then matters are examined and sifted over, in order to support and arm ourselves against the attacks of Satan. The struggles of the old man, also, make us watch and seek, in order to find out the new one; but it is hard to describe him: the head of the new man is knowledge; he is renewed in this, Col. 3:10.

His eyes are the illuminating anointings of the Holy Spirit giving us an understanding, Rev. 3:18; I John 2:27. Without this he sees nothing. His hands are faith and the assurance of it; with these he holds fast, and will not let go, Song 3:4; Gen. 32:26.

His feet are the actings of faith under the influence of the Spirit; if these are continued he can walk, either upon the waves of the sea, or upon the dry land; but, if these fail, he either halts or sinks; and, whichever it be, in he goes; nor will he venture out again unless the sun shine; either mercy, love, or divine power, must influence him and draw him, before he will attempt to stir abroad again. 'We walk by faith (and feeling), not by sight', II Cor. 5:7. I say by feeling: for faith stands in the power of God, and it moves in the same; for we are kept up, and kept on, by the power of God through faith; and without this power their is no walking safely. 'Hold thou me up, and I shall be safe.'

Righteousness is the robe of this new man, and true holiness his glorious adorning. 'And that ye put on the new man, which after God is created in righteousness and true holiness', Eph. 4:24.

This new man, that I am speaking of, is of divine origin, and of heavenly extraction; he is born of the most Holy Spirit of God. 'That which is born of the Spirit is spirit.' This principle of grace, which is called the new man, and is promised in the old testament under the names of a new heart and a new spirit, is that which Peter alludes to when he says, 'Whereby are given unto us exceeding great and precious promises, that by these ye might be partakers of the divine nature', II Peter 1:4. The apostle says that this new man is created after the image of him that created him; and therefore it is a creature, and a very holy creature, being created in righteousness.

The heart of this new man is love, for love influences every member of him; hence we are exhorted to put on charity, the bond of all perfectness, Col. 3:14; which is the same as to put on the new man. Now as love is the fulfilling of the law, both the first and the second table; yea, and the gospel too, for, 'Charity believeth all things'; the apostle says that this new man is created in righteousness. The heart of this new man being love, and love fulfilling both the law and the prophets, love is the righteousness of this new man.

Moreover, as one member of this new man is faith, so of course this new man must believe also. Observe the following text: 'But now is made manifest, and by the scriptures of the prophets, according to the commandment of the everlasting God, made known to all nations for the obedience of faith', Rom. 16:26.

Note here, it is not called the obedience of men, nor is it called our obedience by faith, or obedience in faith, though this may be true; but the obedience here spoken of is faith itself; it is the obedience of faith, and this is the obedience of the new man; and of course he is created in righteousness, having both faith and love, which fulfil both the law of faith and of works, and therefore there is no unrighteousness in this new man.

And this is a truth, that, as in the justification of our persons the righteousness of God by faith of Jesus Christ is imputed, so in the sanctification of our souls there is a righteous nature imparted. He is created in true holiness in opposition to all ceremonial, negative, spurious, counterfeit, or hypocritical holiness, which is nothing but an outward show in the flesh.

Every member of this new man is holy, there is real holiness in every part of him; every grace produced in the soul under the operations of the Holy Spirit is holy; hence this new man is called the holiness of God. God chastens us for our profit, that we might be partakers of his holiness, Heb. 12:10. That is, after our chastisements are over, which are intended to humble us, God giveth us more grace; for he resisteth the proud, but giveth grace unto the humble, James 4:6.

Hence trials make this grace shine the brighter, and appear the more conspicuous; for these are intended to weaken and subdue our inbred corruptions, which lust against the Spirit.

The ornaments of this new man, or that with which he is decked, especially when the believer puts them on and appears at court, are meekness and quietude. 'Whose adorning let it not be the outward adorning of plaiting the hair, and of wearing of gold, or of putting on of apparel; but let it be the hidden man of the heart, in that which is not corruptible, even the ornament of a meek and quiet spirit, which is in the sight of God of great price', I Pet. 3:3,4.

These ornaments are said to be incorruptible. Meekness is a fruit of the Spirit, and exercises itself upon God, after we have been under his chastening hand and are humbled, and the affliction begins to be sanctified to us.

These ornaments are worn for many days together at the soul's first espousal to Christ; and are generally continued, more or less, as long as the wedding lasts and the bridegroom continues to discover his dying love to the bride. 'I will greatly rejoice in the Lord, my soul shall be joyful in my God; for he hath clothed me with the garments of salvation, he hath covered me with the robe of righteousness, as a bridegroom decketh himself with ornaments, and as a bride adorneth herself with her jewels', Isaiah 61:10.

Thus we see that the church ascribes all her attire to her Lord; he provided both wedding dress and heavenly ornaments. He hath clothed us, he hath covered us, and adorned us like a bride with her jewels.

Meekness is generally put on upon every undeserved visit that the Lord pays us, especially when he restores our souls from our backslidings, or reclaims us from our misdoings, appears in our behalf in times of trouble, or when he gives us a fresh sight and sense of our interest after some sad days of doubting and fearing. Nay, we never think ourselves, on such occasions, properly dressed without these jewels; these generally attend the kisses that make all up, for they are a satisfactory proof to us of the renewals of love.

Moreover, sore trials contract the heart; and under these contractions a load of grief is conceived, and the heart gets full, and must have vent. Under such circumstances, if legal bondage and a sense of wrath operate, these beget slavish fear; at such times the lips often ease the heart by muttering perverseness, which only hardens and makes the breach wider: but, when meekness operates, all the ashes are poured out at the foot of the altar.

The other jewel is quietness; this springs from fulness, and all fulness of satisfaction in us is according to faith; 'In quietness and confidence shall be your strength.' Faith puts on a perfect and an all-sufficient righteousness, and fills the soul with joy and peace in believing in it. 'The effect of righteousness is quietness and assurance for ever', Isa. 32:17. And the stronger faith is, the more solid the joy; full assurance of faith is fulness of satisfaction; and full satisfaction produces quietude, and sets us down with contentment, thankful for what we have, and envying none.

But this jewel is only worn by the bride whilst she abides with her bridegroom. 'My people shall dwell in a peaceable habitation, and in sure dwellings, and in quiet resting-places.' Our quiet resting-places are in the electing love of God the Father, the finished salvation of Christ, and in the work and witness of the Holy Ghost. The soul that is ignorant of these, is like the troubled sea which cannot rest. But my brethren will say, Can the Holy Trinity, with any degree of propriety, be called a place and a resting-place? Yes. 'LORD, thou hast been our dwelling place in all generations', Psalm 90:1. And I know of no rest nor resting-places for weary souls but these.

The bowels of this new man are described by the apostle; for, whenever the old man is put off and the new man is put on, some of the following things appear. 'Put on, therefore, as the elect of God, holy and beloved, bowels of mercies, kindness, humbleness of mind, meekness, longsuffering', Col. 3:12.

Bowels of mercies are exercised chiefly towards the children of God in trouble, and flow from the influence of love and sympathy; and are only exercised by those who know what soul distresses are. Kindness is a grace that springs from tenderness, and tenderness springs from life. Souls quickened by the Spirit have keen sensations and tender feelings, which a child of God in distress will easily touch; for grace in one soul claims kindred with grace in another, and will move in consort with it. If one subject of grace suffer, the other suffers; if one be honoured the other will rejoice; the motions of it will make us weep with them that weep, and rejoice with them that do rejoice.

This humbleness of mind, meekness and longsuffering, the apostle ascribes altogether to charity, which is the very heart and soul of the new man, and the choicest principle to be found in him. 'Charity suffereth long, and is kind; charity envieth not; charity vaunteth not itself, is not puffed up, doth not behave itself unseemly, seeketh not her own, is not easily provoked, thinketh no evil; rejoiceth not in iniquity, but rejoiceth in the truth', I Cor. 13:4-6.

The daily employ of this new man is hoping and expecting to return to his own native country. Grace shall reign through righteousness unto eternal life, by Jesus Christ our Lord, Rom. 5:21. And in this hope and expectation it exercises much patience and longsuffering till it be obtained; for, 'If we hope for that we see not, then do we with patience wait for it.'

The spiritual ears of the new man are very wonderful, and cannot be described. But this is a truth: God speaks many words by the Spirit to the soul, or speaks friendly to the church's heart, Hosea 2:14. And what the Lord speaks is not only felt, but heard and understood, although no sound reaches the ear or the body. Paul, when caught up into paradise, heard unspeakable words, which it was not possible to utter; and yet he doth not know whether the body was in company or not.

To infuse and form this new man in the soul is the work of the Holy Spirit, and so is every renewal and every revival of him, from his first formation till perfection in endless glory takes place. 'The LORD will perfect that which concerneth me: thy mercy, O LORD, endureth for ever: forsake not the works of thine own hands', Psalm 138:8.

How sensibly felt are the revivals of this good work under the operations of the Holy Ghost! Sometimes by communicating fresh power, all on a sudden, when everything seems to be falling to decay, and the poor believer is just ready to cast away all confidence, and in his own mind to fall a victim to sin and Satan, concluding all to be lost for ever; then is the divine power of the Spirit put forth in this new creature. 'That he would grant you, according to the riches of his glory, to be strengthened with might by his Spirit in the inner man', Eph. 3:16.

Sometimes great communications of light, and fresh discoveries of the love of God in Christ, wonderfully strengthen and inflame the new man. 'But mine horn shalt thou exalt like the horn of an unicorn: I shall be anointed with fresh oil', Psalm 92:10.

At other times the uncommon struggles of hope attended with vigour, earnestness, diligence, liveliness, activity, and anxiety after the glory that is to be revealed, appear in this new man. 'Now the God of hope fill you with all joy and peace in believing, that ye may abound in hope, through the power of the Holy Ghost', Rom. 15:13.

Every day, throughout the believer's whole pilgrimage, does the Holy Spirit revive or renew this new man of grace in one member or another; as it is written, 'For all things are for your sakes, that the abundant grace might through the thanksgiving of many redound to the glory of God. For which cause we faint not; but, though our outward man perish, yet the inward man is renewed day by day', II Cor. 4:15,16.

'That which is born of the Spirit is spirit.' Now it is against the Holy Ghost, in his forming and preserving this new man which is born of the Spirit, that the flesh lusteth. 'For the flesh lusteth against the Spirit, and the Spirit against the flesh: and these are contrary the one to the other; so that ye cannot do the things that ye would. But, if ye be led by the Spirit, ye are not under the law', Gal. 5:17,18.

The way that the Spirit leads us is by influencing and putting fresh strength, life, love, and fervour, in the new man. This new man of grace is a mighty worker, while the Spirit keeps renewing him. 'I laboured', says Paul, 'more abundantly than they all; yet not I, but the grace of God which was with me.'

Sometimes we have noble works ascribed to the different members of the new man. We read of the work of faith, and labour of love, and patience of hope, in our Lord Jesus Christ, I Thess. 1:3. Sometimes faith appears very strong, and performs wonders, especially in times of great need; as we can see in David, when he went against the giant of Gath. At other times love labours mightily both to the Lord and to his people: the first may be seen in Mary at the Lord's feet, and the second in Paul to the Corinthians. At other times the patience of hope is very conspicuous in waiting for that which is hoped for. 'I will wait upon the LORD, that hideth his face from Jacob, and I will look for him', Isa. 8:17.

This new man of grace comes from the fulness of Christ, in whom all fulness dwells, and out of whose fulness we all receive, and grace for grace. And it is the Spirit that works in us by his wonderful operation, and he supplies this new man daily; hence we read of a supply of the Spirit of Jesus Christ, Phil. 1:19; that is, the Spirit of Christ supplies us with more grace from Christ, the blessed Head of influence.

'Now', says the apostle, 'if ye be led by the Spirit, ye are not under the law.' They that are under the law have nothing else but lust and corruption working in them, let them talk of spurious holiness as much as they please. 'Law was given', says Milton, 'to evince man's natural pravity, by stirring up sin against law to fight.' 'The motions of sins, which were by the law (stirred up), did work in our members to bring forth fruit unto death', Rom. 7:5. So that he who is under the law is destitute of that new man, and of course has nothing but sin in him.

He will at times feel rebukes, checks, and lashes within; which he may, and many do, call the old man of sin; but this is a mistake; it is not an enemy, but a friend; not the old man of sin, but honest conscience doing his duty, buffeting the sinner for his hypocrisy. So, on the other hand, a hypocrite, will, at times, find a little calm of peace and tranquillity in his mind, which he may call the new man, and I believe thousands do so; but, as the former is nothing but natural conscience accusing, so the latter is nothing but natural conscience excusing, according to the light of nature.

For, even under this calm of peace and tranquillity, there is no godly sorrow flowing out to God; no condemning, hating, and abhorring self; nor any real tears of pious grief, mourning over a suffering Saviour; no repentance towards the Lord, nor heartfelt gratitude to him, nor real thanks and praises for his longsuffering, undeserved, and unexpected clemency.

Such men's peace springs from a cessation of arms with Satan; they have had a few days respite, in which the devil has not wallowed them in the mire; and, during this interval, they have done something for God, and of course he must be pleased with them.

All this takes its spring from self, and centres in self, and there such faith stands; for he has no trust but in his own heart; look to Jesus he cannot, because there is no good thing in him toward the Lord God: whereas the believer looks to Jesus, depends on his arm, and views his own heart worse than Satan himself, deceitful above all things, and desperately wicked, Jer. 17:9.

The believer knows that he can stand no longer than while the Lord upholds him; if he withdraw his supporting hand he is sure to sink, and when sunk he despairs of all help in his own arm, or in his own heart; he knows that nothing can recover him but a propitious look from his dear Lord, or a restoring visit from him or a fresh discovery by faith of his dying love, attended with the reviving and renewing operations of the Holy Spirit of promise.

'The flesh lusteth against the Spirit', in behalf of, and to be gratified in, its own delightful fruits; which the apostle mentions: which are, 'Adultery, fornication, uncleanness, lasciviousness, idolatry, witchcraft, hatred, variance, emulations, wrath, strife, seditions, heresies, envyings, murders, drunkenness, revellings, and such like:' Gal. 5:19-21.

Some of these are sins which easily beset the child of God; they often intrude themselves into his mind; yea, even when he would do good some of these are present with him: nor is the believer without his slips and falls in one way or other. But still he is not a servant of sin; for they that are the servants of sin, are free from righteousness, Rom. 6:20. Such are free in sin, and free from all righteousness; which the believer never is. He is a servant of righteousness, and doth serve both in faith and love.

And, though he does not live without sin, being in one sense still in the flesh; yet sin is neither his element nor his service. 'For, though we walk in the flesh, we do not war after the flesh', II Cor. 10:3, but war against it.

Nor are the sins of believers called service, for they have no wages for it, neither present pleasure nor endless death, which are all the wages that a servant of sin gets. He may be brought into captivity to the law of sin, which is in his members, Rom. 7:23; but a captive and a servant in this matter widely differ.

The apostle, having called the whole mass of inbred corruptions both the old nature of the flesh, and a body of sin, also assigns different sins as so many different members of this hateful body, in allusion to the body of a man. 'Mortify, therefore, your members which are upon the earth; fornication, uncleanness, inordinate affection, evil concupiscence, and covetousness, which is idolatry', Col. 3:5.

So, on the other hand, he calls the principle of implanted grace the new man. And, as this new man is formed by the Holy Spirit, and consists of different graces, so the apostle calls these the fruits of the Spirit in opposition to the other, which he calls the works of the flesh. 'But the fruit of the Spirit is love, joy, peace, longsuffering, gentleness, goodness, faith, meekness, temperance: against such there is no law', Gal. 5:22,23.

Now all these, strictly speaking, are not graces of the Spirit; but fruits and effects of his operation: for gentleness, longsuffering, and temperance, may be exercised, and often are exercised, by men in a state of nature. Some, who are inured to sufferings, may and do suffer with much patience; others are naturally temperate; and some are gentle, easy, and unmoved, who have no fear of God before their eyes. But those whose nature is the opposite of these, are made so by grace. When the wolf is taught to dwell with the lamb, and the lion to lie down with the kid, then these things are attended to, and men exercise themselves in them in the fear of God.

Nor are all the graces or fruits of the Spirit mentioned in this place. Fear, patience, zeal, and hope, are fruits of the Spirit; and so are contrition, godly sorrow, humility, and repentance.

Now, as the new man is composed of these manifold graces, so the Holy Spirit, by his powerful operations, enlivens, strengthens, and draws forth into exercise, first one and then another, as seemeth good to him. Sometimes he strengthens faith, and fortifies the mind with such might and power, that the excellency and the power appear so conspicuously to be of God, that the man is quite above himself. 'But truly I am full of power by the Spirit of the LORD, and of judgment, and of might, to declare unto Jacob his transgression, and to Israel his sin', Micah 3:8.

Again, when we are led to defend any truth that is opposed, and it pleases the Holy Spirit to instruct, settle, and establish the children of God in them, he not only gives light into the truth, bringing text after text to the mind to support and confirm it, but he fires the soul with such zeal, that it is clad with it as with a cloak. 'My zeal hath consumed me; because mine enemies have forgotten thy words. Thy word is very pure: therefore thy servant loveth it', Psalm 119:139,140.

At other times faith is influenced with such power and activity, that the soul can tell beforehand something of the success that shall attend the word. 'When, therefore, I have performed this, and have sealed to them this fruit, I will come by you into Spain. And I am sure that when I come unto you, I shall come in the fulness of the blessing of the gospel of Christ.'

Sometimes one grace shall appear predominant, and sometimes another; as patience in Job; meekness in Moses; godly sorrow in Hannah; jealousy for God's honour in Elijah; contrition in David; and love in Paul: 'I am not only ready to be bound, but even to die at Jerusalem for the name of the Lord Jesus.'

All these move and act as the Holy Spirit operates in them; he enlivens and invigorates them; but, without divine inspiration, there is neither motion nor emission. 'Awake, O north wind; and come, thou south; blow upon my garden, that the spices thereof may flow out. Let my beloved come into his garden, and eat his pleasant fruits', Song 4:16.

If my dearly beloved brethren will observe these things they will perceive much more than I can describe; and they will find the different frames into which they are cast to be wonderfully suited to the work then in hand.

To the Thessalonians Paul was a nurse; to Timothy an affectionate father; to the Corinthians God made him the personification of humility and meekness; to the false apostles he was an invincible champion; to the weak a babe in grace; to the Jews straitened as under the law; to the Gentiles as one guided alone by conscience; to the wise and discerning he was the chiefest apostle; and to Alexander and Elymas the sorcerer he was a lion. 'I am made all things to all men, that I might by all means save some.'

Well may the apostle say there are diversities of operations; for they are diverse, and innumerable too; yea, and often various in one day. Life, contrition, and sorrow, for morning prayer; a sweet flow of gratitude soon after for a thank-offering; upon the back of this comes a promise in due season, increasing faith; then a smiling providence turns up, that makes the bowels yearn; next comes a letter bringing good tidings, and blessing God for the instrument, and for the power of divine grace put forth; this fires the soul with fresh zeal for the work. Then comes a poor soul telling the dreadful tale of the plague of leprosy breaking out in the house; these touch one's love and sympathy.

Next comes in a word, opening out a large field of hidden treasures, pearls and jewels for Zion. And, last of all, comes in an arch hypocrite, appearing to be some great one, when he is nothing, with all the art and craft imaginable to impose upon the judgment; and, with his appearance, comes the word, 'What have I to do with thee? Get thee to the prophets of thy father, and to the prophets of thy mother. But now bring me a minstrel', II Kings 3:13,15.

Let my dear brethren observe these things, and they will have some insight into this blessed promise; 'I the LORD do keep it; I will water it every moment: lest any hurt it, I will keep it night and day', Isaiah 27:3.

The new man is fed by prayer, by reading, by meditation, by hearing the word, and by conversing with the lively friends of the bridegroom. He is very choice in his food. Hence it appears that, under the dry orations which are drawn from the letter, and those confused jumbles upon free will, enforced by those who have not been emptied of self, but are settled upon their lees; and those violent shouts from the top of the mountain, not of Zion, but of Sinai: none of these entertain the new man; it is not such tidings as these that bring him, nor does the Spirit, who forms him, accompany such. God gives testimony to the word of his grace.

The new man feeds upon power. You read of strength by the Spirit's might in the inward man; you read of his being renewed day by day, and of his being renewed in knowledge after the image of him that created him. Light, attended with love, feeds him; it revives him, refreshes him, and renews him.

He gathers his myrrh with his spice. Myrrh is a bitter potion to the old man, but it never hurts the new one. Spice comes after the myrrh has had the desired effect. But this sweet scent is no more pleasing to the old man than the myrrh; the bitterness of trials mortify the old man, and so do the sweet odours of humbling grace. The new man eats his honeycomb with his honey, and drinks his wine with his milk, Song 5:1.

The promises, and the sweets that are hid in them; divine love, and the comforts that attend it; are the sweet provisions of the new man. The old man, with all his members, Paul describes; and those very evil things of which he is composed are the things that feed, entertain, and gratify him. When he is fed, then the new man is starved, and leanness enters into the soul.

Of the manifold graces infused and wrought in the soul by the Holy Spirit the new man is composed, and by those very things of which he is composed, is he fed. His divine origin is God, and therefore called the divine nature. His mansion is Christ Jesus, in whom all fulness of grace dwells, and from whose fulness all grace is received.

Fresh supplies from the same fulness by the Holy Ghost feed him and keep him alive; and under no other preaching than that preaching of Christ; and it must be Christ revealed and made known in the soul of the preacher. Under such, and under no other, can this new man be fed and nourished; and this many know by sad experience, who are seeking water and there is none, and their tongues are failing for thirst.

'Now unto him that is able to keep you from falling, and to present you faultless before the presence of his glory with exceeding joy; to the only wise God our Saviour, be glory and majesty, dominion and power, both now and ever. Amen.'

the nineteenth meditation

XIX

The Nineteenth Meditation

AND now I shall proceed further with my subject, which is to show, next,

That the Holy Spirit in the gospel must be obeyed; for, according to the obedience of man is the reward to be given, whether of sin unto death or of obedience unto righteousness. 'Be not deceived; God is not mocked: for, whatsoever a man soweth, that shall he also reap. For he that soweth to his flesh shall of the flesh reap corruption; but he that soweth to the Spirit shall of the Spirit reap life everlasting. And let us not be weary in well doing: for in due season we shall reap, if we faint not. As we have therefore opportunity, let us do good unto all men, especially unto them who are of the household of faith', Gal. 6:7-10.

To sow to the Spirit is to obey him and to be led by him. Our Lord calls himself a sower, and the word of life which he sowed he calls seed; and in sowing the good seed of the word he was obedient to him that appointed him. 'My Father gave me a commandment what I should say and what I should speak, and I know that his commandment is life everlasting: whatsoever I speak, therefore, even as the Father said unto me, so I speak', John 12:49,50.

Now there is a twofold sowing to the Spirit: internal and external. Internal, when we observe his operations, and are obedient to his motions and dictates; for instance, when he applies the word with power, and reproves us with the word, convincing us of our sins. Then for a person to speak evil of the preacher by whom the Spirit speaks, to rail against him and the truth, is hating the light, and rebelling against it and against our own convictions of the truth of it; and this rebellion is against the Holy Ghost himself. It is said of Israel, in the wilderness, that, 'They rebelled and vexed his holy Spirit; therefore he was turned to be their enemy, and he fought against them', Isaiah 63:10.

Moses and Aaron were God's mouth to the people; the Holy Spirit spake in them to the children of Israel: but, 'They envied Moses in the camp, and Aaron the saint of the Lord.' And by their rebelling against these men they rebelled against the Holy Spirit which influenced them and spoke by them. 'They angered him also at the waters of strife, so that it went ill with Moses for their sakes: because they provoked his spirit, so that he spake unadvisedly with his lips', Psalm 106:16,32,33.

Sinners, reproved and convinced by the Holy Spirit, should not only come to the light and be diligent in their attendance on the word; but God calls for confessions to be made to him, and for submission to his will; which is called humbling ourselves under the mighty hand of God, that he may exalt us in due time.

There is such a thing as accepting the punishment of our iniquity, choosing the chastenings of God before our own will and our own way; saying, as others have done, 'Search me and try me, and see if there be any wicked way in me, and lead me in the way everlasting.' And again, 'I will bear the indignation of the Lord, because I have sinned against him, until he plead my cause and execute judgment for me; he will bring me forth to the light, and I shall behold his righteousness.' Coming to the light that our deeds may be made manifest; exposing our conscience to the force and power of his word, however sharp and piercing; confessing all our crimes, which the light of the word discovers and reproves us for; is accepting our punishment, and preferring the chastisements of God before carnal ease and the pleasures of sin, and is yielding obedience to the Holy Spirit; and it shows that the heart is made honest.

The Spirit is a spirit of supplication. He sets the elect of God to crying day and night, until God avenge them of their adversaries. 'Call upon me in the time of trouble', says God; 'I will deliver thee, and thou shalt glorify me.' And again, 'I will bring the third part through the fire, and will refine them as silver is refined, and try them as gold is tried; they shall call upon my name, and I will hear them; I will say, It is my people; and they shall say, the Lord is my God.'

This should be carefully and diligently attended to when the Holy Spirit is illuminating, quickening, reproving, and convincing the sinner; and, if it is neglected, the Spirit resents it, and makes conscience accuse the sinner for this his neglect, and he is often covered with shame and confusion of face when he goes to the throne of grace again. Nor is it seldom that some disaster or other befalls the sensible sinner, under this sin of omission, when prayer has been neglected; and oftentimes the sinner is informed of this when he comes to examine himself.

Prayer, in the times of the gospel, was typified by the offering of incense under the law, which was perpetual morning and evening; and prayer goes by the same name under the gospel. 'For from the rising of the sun even unto the going down of the same my name shall be great among the Gentiles; and in every place incense shall be offered unto my name, and a pure offering; for my name shall be great among the heathen, saith the Lord of hosts', Mal. 1:11.

Moreover, God requires of us thank-offerings for favours received. 'I will make her wilderness like Eden, and her desert like the garden of the LORD; joy and gladness shall be found therein, thanksgiving and the voice of melody.' The souls of God's saints are often filled with joy and gladness, that thanksgiving and the voice of melody may redound to the glory of God, by humble acknowledgments of his mercies, and by singing his praises.

Furthermore, we should celebrate those perfections of God which shine so bright in his appointment of Christ Jesus to be the Saviour of mankind; which is done by speaking good, or by making honourable mention, of his holy name; and by proclaiming the glorious perfections of his nature, making them famous and illustrious among mankind; praising and commending the holy properties of his nature; and enumerating and extolling them, by speaking of his manifold and wonderful works, and of the innumerable mercies and blessings of his providence and grace towards us in Christ Jesus.

The scriptures abound with such ascriptions, acclamations, and celebrations, in the saints' holy triumphs. David is famous for this; there is scarce a revealed attribute of God but he makes honourable mention of.

As holiness. 'God hath spoken in his holiness, I will rejoice.'

Power. 'Sing unto the LORD a new song, for his right hand and his holy arm hath gotten him the victory.'

His might and reign, his glory and majesty. 'Great is the LORD, and greatly to be praised; and his greatness is unsearchable. One generation shall praise thy works to another, and shall declare thy mighty acts. I will speak of the glorious honour of thy majesty, and of thy wondrous works. And men shall speak of the might of thy terrible acts: and I will declare thy greatness. They shall abundantly utter the memory of thy great goodness, and shall sing of thy righteousness. All thy works shall praise thee, O LORD; and thy saints shall bless thee. They shall speak of the glory of thy kingdom, and talk of thy power; to make known to the sons of men his mighty acts, and the glorious majesty of his kingdom', Psalm 145:3-12.

Almost every perfection of the Divine Being is brought forth in the holy triumphs of the royal psalmist, justice and judgment not excepted. 'Justice and judgment are the habitation of his throne; mercy and truth shall go before thy face.' Of lovingkindness David sings; of faithfulness and truth; of goodness, pity, and compassion; and of mercy, and the eternal duration of it, throughout a whole psalm.

Different frames and different dispensations call for different offerings and exercises. 'Is any afflicted? let him pray.' Times of trouble and times of affliction in the furnace are seasons for extraordinary prayers; the common morning and evening sacrifices are not sufficient at such times; we must give ourselves unto prayer; give up ourselves wholly unto it, and attend to this very thing.

Nor will the old common way, no, nor even the usual mode of expressions, do. Fiery trials call for fresh power, and even for agonizing energy; new words, arguments, and unusual pleas and entreaties must be made use of; our arguments and pathetic pleadings must tally with our dreadful sensations.

Souls that meditate terror must fetch their words from their feelings, or else the words of their mouth will run counter to the meditations of their heart.

We must use all our skill in utterance of distress, grief and sorrow, and all the eloquence of misery. 'I cried to thee, O LORD; and unto the LORD I made supplication. What profit is there in my blood, when I go down to the pit? Shall the dust praise thee? shall it declare thy truth?' Psalm 30:8,9. 'Will the Lord cast off for ever? and will he be favourable no more? Is his mercy clean gone for ever? doth his promise fail for evermore? Hath God forgotten to be gracious? Hath he in anger shut up his tender mercies?' Psalm 77:7-9. 'For the grave cannot praise thee; death cannot celebrate thee: they that go down into the pit cannot hope for thy truth.'

As times of affliction are praying times, or times to give ourselves unto prayer; so times of prosperity are times of praise, for thanksgiving, and for singing with grace in our hearts, making melody to the Lord. If we would sow to the Spirit we must observe these things; and likewise shun all damnable heresies, which have the least tendency to depreciate the Son of God, or to eclipse his glory, or lessen him in our esteem or affections.

The Holy Spirit is both the testifier and the glorifier of Christ, and he will never countenance any low, mean, unworthy or unbecoming conceptions of him. I am not speaking of the evil suggestions or fiery darts of Satan, which we cannot help, and which are Satan's sins and not ours; but of those damnable principles and sentiments which some men hold, and which divest the Saviour of all the glory and majesty of deity, and debase him to the level of a mere creature, which is what God the Holy Ghost will ever resist and resent.

Sowing to the Spirit internally, is to walk as the Spirit leads us; he is to guide us into all truth, and not to speak of himself. This chiefly respects our principles, the object of our faith and worship, and the true and spiritual worship and adoration which God requires of us; the whole of which is included in what the scripture calls the way of holiness, Isaiah 35:8; which is following the Lord in the regeneration, Mt. 19:28. In which following all things become new; not only a new birth, but we are brought into the bond of a new covenant, are made to serve in the newness of Spirit, with new views and new principles, and to walk in a new and living way.

The Spirit leads us to walk with God in peace and equity. These two, peace and equity, always go together. When the believer keeps a conscience void of offence, he delights himself in the abundance of peace; he makes straight paths for his feet, and he finds his ways to be pleasantness and his paths peace. But, if he make a crooked path, and all the ways of sin are crooked, because they are counter to the will and word of God, he that goes therein shall not know peace.

Secondly, there is a sowing to the Spirit externally. And the apostle's explanation of this sowing to the Spirit is given by himself. 'Let us not be weary in well doing; for in due season we shall reap if we faint not.' And then tells us what he means by well doing. 'As we have therefore opportunity, let us do good unto all men, especially unto them who are of the household of faith', Gal. 6:9,10.

To do good to them that are not as yet in the faith, is to labour to recommend Christ and his gospel to them by a becoming life and conversation, to drop a word of reproof or instruction to them when opportunity offers, or to use our endeavours to bring them under the word. 'And the Spirit and the bride say, Come. And let him that heareth say, Come. And let him that is athirst come. And whosoever will, let him take the water of life freely', Rev. 22:17.

After our Lord had called two or three of his first followers, he made use of these to bring others. Andrew, hearing and seeing John point to Christ, followed him; he then finds his brother Peter, and brings him to Jesus; the next day Jesus found Philip; and then Philip finds Nathanael and brings him: and, blessed be God, this work is going on still.

Moreover, by doing good unto all men, the apostle means liberality. Poor people have more exalted notions of alms-deeds than they have of any other good work whatsoever. You may talk to them about faith, and about love to the brotherhood, and the patience of hope, and of suffering afflictions, of bearing the cross, and of self-denial, but these are all out of their sight and out of their reach: but circumspection in life and a liberal heart are obvious to all, and stop the mouths of all, unless it be the devil himself.

And in this the child of God has a double advantage. The world loves its own; sinners love sinners, and will give and lend to sinners; but sinners cannot love saints as saints, and because they belong to Christ; nor can they relieve them, or be charitable to them, because of God's love to them in Christ Jesus. 'When saw we thee an hungered, or athirst, or a stranger, or naked, or sick, or in prison, and did not minister unto thee?' The answer is, 'Insomuch as ye did it not to one of the least of these (my brethren) ye did it not to me.'

Not one of all these ever relieved a child of God as such; whereas there are thousands of sinners, persecutors, and even enemies, both to God and to his church, who do partake largely of the liberality of the people of God; and this is acceptable to God, as may be seen in the prayers and alms of Cornelius the centurion, Acts 10; and in the nobleness of mind which Abraham showed to the king of Sodom.

By these means some are drawn or won to hear the word of God, and that to profit. The mouths of others are stopped, while the believer makes it manifest that the kingdom, of which he is a subject, is not of this world. And in all these things God is glorified: and the children of God are a sweet savour unto him, both in them that perish and in them that are saved. 'Let your light so shine before men that they may see your good works, and glorify your Father which is in heaven.'

But the apostle adds, 'Especially to the household of faith.' The ties of nature give us a feeling for those who are in the flesh, and fill us with wonder at discriminating grace, when the bond of all perfectness binds us more strongly to the excellent of the earth; for we can only pity the other, but we can delight ourselves in these.

To the household of faith, if we sow sparingly, we shall reap sparingly, and if we sow bountifully we shall reap bountifully. To receive a prophet in the name of a prophet, has the promise of a prophet's reward. To receive a righteous man in the name of a righteous man, has the promise of a righteous man's reward. And he that receives one of the little ones that belong to Christ, shall in no wise lose his reward. A morsel of bread, or a cup of cold water only, given to any in the name of a disciple, shall most surely be rewarded at the resurrection of the just; for, 'He that soweth to the Spirit shall of the Spirit reap life everlasting.'

We must sow prayers in their behalf; we may sow the seeds of instruction in their ears, bread and water to their bellies, apparel to their backs, and relief in their necessities; and reap fourfold in this life, and in the world to come life everlasting. To all this the word of God directs, and to all this the Holy Spirit leads; 'For the fruit of the Spirit is in all goodness, and righteousness, and truth', Eph. 5:9.

Once more. The best of men have no more than their own appointed time on the earth; the strength, the natural and spiritual abilities, the grace, and such worldly substance as it pleases God to give them. Now, as all these come of God through Christ, so from all these things Christ expects some returns; for, when he comes, it will be to know what every one has gained by trading.

Some redeem the time while the days are evil. Paul was willing to spend and be spent for the church; he spent his property and his strength in the service of Christ; with the grace that he had received by the Spirit he seasoned many; and by his natural and spiritual abilities he became all things to all men; he instructed many, he silenced many gainsayers, and left a glorious testimony behind of his fruitfulness in the church, of the goodness of God to him, of the blessedness of his state, and of his glorious and triumphant end: and in all these things he sowed to the Spirit; and they that do so shall of the Spirit reap life everlasting.

This reaping respects this present life as well as the future. God's blessing upon mount Zion is life for evermore. And it has pleased God to put the blessing of life into every spiritual thing that the believer deals in. Upon his believing he passes from death to life; his repentance is unto life; the promises he obtains are the words of life; his justification is unto life; God circumcises his heart to love God, that he may live; his hope is a lively hope; and the very way in which he walks is the new and living way.

In short, the love and eternal purpose of God, the voice of the Son, and the operations of the Spirit, are all life to the believer; and the more we sow the more we reap; the more we love God and the brethren, the more lively we are; the stronger our faith and the firmer our hope are, the more abundant is our life.

In all these things lie our sowing and reaping. And let us, my dear brethren, be constant, unmoveable, and always abounding in this work of the Lord, knowing that our labour is not, shall not be, in vain in the Lord. To get weary and to faint in well doing, is sad work. 'Look to yourselves', says John, 'that we lose not those things which we have wrought, but that we receive a full reward', II John 8.

The grace of our Lord Jesus Christ, the love of God our heavenly Father, and the communion of the Spirit of all grace, be with you, and with all that love our Lord Jesus Christ in sincerity and truth, both now and for evermore, is the prayer of your companion in travail.

INDEX

TO OTHER PUBLICATIONS

PSALMS, HYMNS AND SPIRITUAL SONGS

THE PSALMS
OF THE
OLD TESTAMENT

The Psalms of the Old Testament, the result of years of painstaking labour, is an original translation into verse from the Authorised Version, which seeks to present the Psalms in the purest scriptural form possible for singing. Here, for the first time, divine names are rendered as and when they occur in the scripture, the distinction between LORD and Lord has been preserved, and every essential point of doctrine and experience appears with unique perception and fidelity.

The Psalms of the Old Testament is the first part of a trilogy written by John Metcalfe, the second part of which is entitled *Spiritual Songs from the Gospels*, and the last, *The Hymns of the New Testament*. These titles provide unique and accurate metrical versions of passages from the psalms, the gospels and the new testament epistles respectively, and are intended to be used together in the worship of God.

Price £2.50 *(postage extra)*
(hard-case binding, dust-jacket)
ISBN 0 9506366 7 3

SPIRITUAL SONGS
FROM
THE GOSPELS

The *Spiritual Songs from the Gospels*, the result of years of painstaking labour, is an original translation into verse from the Authorised Version, which seeks to present essential parts of the gospels in the purest scriptural form possible for singing. The careful selection from Matthew, Mark, Luke and John, set forth in metrical verse of the highest integrity, enables the singer to sing 'the word of Christ' as if from the scripture itself, 'richly and in all wisdom'; and, above all, in a way that facilitates worship in song of unprecedented fidelity.

The *Spiritual Songs from the Gospels* is the central part of a trilogy written by John Metcalfe, the first part of which is entitled *The Psalms of the Old Testament*, and the last, *The Hymns of the New Testament*. These titles provide unique and accurate metrical versions of passages from the psalms, the gospels and the new testament epistles respectively, and are intended to be used together in the worship of God.

Price £2.50 *(postage extra)*
(hard-case binding, dust-jacket)
ISBN 0 9506366 8 1

THE HYMNS
OF THE
NEW TESTAMENT

The *Hymns of the New Testament*, the result of years of painstaking labour, is an original translation into verse from the Authorised Version, which presents essential parts of the new testament epistles in the purest scriptural form possible for singing. The careful selection from the book of Acts to that of Revelation, set forth in metrical verse of the highest integrity, enables the singer to sing 'the word of Christ' as if from the scripture itself, 'richly and in all wisdom'; and, above all, in a way that facilitates worship in song of unprecedented fidelity.

The *Hymns of the New Testament* is the last part of a trilogy written by John Metcalfe, the first part of which is entitled *The Psalms of the Old Testament*, and the next, *Spiritual Songs from the Gospels.* These titles provide unique and accurate metrical versions of passages from the psalms, the gospels and the new testament epistles respectively, and are intended to be used together in the worship of God.

Price £2.50 *(postage extra)*
(hard-case binding, dust-jacket)
ISBN 0 9506366 9 X

'THE APOSTOLIC FOUNDATION OF THE CHRISTIAN CHURCH' SERIES

FOUNDATIONS UNCOVERED

THE APOSTOLIC FOUNDATION
OF THE
CHRISTIAN CHURCH

Volume I

Foundations Uncovered is a small book of some 37 pages. This is the introduction to the major series: 'The Apostolic Foundation of the Christian Church'.

Rich in truth, the Introduction deals comprehensively with the foundation of the apostolic faith under the descriptive titles: The Word, The Doctrine, The Truth, The Gospel, The Faith, The New Testament, and The Foundation.

The contents of the book reveal: The Fact of the Foundation; The Foundation Uncovered; What the Foundation is not; How the Foundation is Described; and, Being Built upon the Foundation.

'This book comes with the freshness of a new Reformation.'

Price 30p *(postage extra)*
(Laminated cover)
ISBN 0 9506366 5 7

THE BIRTH OF JESUS CHRIST

THE APOSTOLIC FOUNDATION
OF THE
CHRISTIAN CHURCH

Volume II

'The very spirit of adoration and worship rings through the pages of *The Birth of Jesus Christ.*

'The author expresses with great clarity the truths revealed to him in his study of holy scriptures at depth. We are presented here with a totally lofty view of the Incarnation.

'John Metcalfe is to be classed amongst the foremost expositors of our age; and his writings have about them that quality of timelessness that makes me sure they will one day take their place among the heritage of truly great Christian works.'

From a review by Rev. David Catterson.

'Uncompromisingly faithful to scripture ... has much to offer which is worth serious consideration ... deeply moving.'

The Expository Times.

Price 95p *(postage extra)*
(Laminated Cover)
ISBN 0 9502515 5 0

THE MESSIAH

THE APOSTOLIC FOUNDATION
OF THE
CHRISTIAN CHURCH

Volume III

The Messiah is a spiritually penetrating and entirely original exposition of Matthew chapter one to chapter seven from the trenchant pen of John Metcalfe.

Matthew Chapters One to Seven

Genealogy · Birth · Star of Bethlehem
Herod · Flight to Egypt · Nazareth
John the Baptist · The Baptist's Ministry
Jesus' Baptism · All righteousness Fulfilled
Heaven Opened · The Spirit's Descent
The Temptation of Jesus in the Wilderness
Jesus' Manifestation · The Calling · The True Disciples
The Beatitudes · The Sermon on the Mount

'Something of the fire of the ancient Hebrew prophet .... Metcalfe has spiritual and expository potentials of a high order.'

The Life of Faith.

Price £2.45 *(postage extra)*
(425 pages, Laminated Cover)
ISBN 0 9502515 8 5

THE SON OF GOD AND SEED OF DAVID

THE APOSTOLIC FOUNDATION
OF THE
CHRISTIAN CHURCH

Volume IV

The Son of God and Seed of David is the fourth volume in the major work entitled 'The Apostolic Foundation of the Christian Church.'

'The author proceeds to open and allege that Jesus Christ is and ever was *The Son of God.* This greatest of subjects, this most profound of all mysteries, is handled with reverence and with outstanding perception.

'The second part considers *The Seed of David.* What is meant precisely by 'the seed'? And why 'of David'? With prophetic insight the author expounds these essential verities.'

Price £6.95 *(postage extra)*
Hardback 250 pages
Laminated bookjacket
ISBN 1 870039 16 5

CHRIST CRUCIFIED

THE APOSTOLIC FOUNDATION
OF THE
CHRISTIAN CHURCH

Volume V

Christ Crucified the definitive work on the crucifixion, the blood, and the cross of Jesus Christ.

The crucifixion of Jesus Christ witnessed in the Gospels: the gospel according to Matthew; Mark; Luke; John.

The blood of Jesus Christ declared in the Epistles: the shed blood; the blood of purchase; redemption through his blood; the blood of sprinkling; the blood of the covenant.

The doctrine of the cross revealed in the apostolic foundation of the Christian church: the doctrine of the cross; the cross and the body of sin; the cross and the carnal mind; the cross and the law; the offence of the cross; the cross of our Lord Jesus Christ.

Price £6.95 *(postage extra)*
Hardback 300 pages
Laminated bookjacket
ISBN 1 870039 08 4

JUSTIFICATION BY FAITH

THE APOSTOLIC FOUNDATION
OF THE
CHRISTIAN CHURCH

Volume VI

THE HEART OF THE GOSPEL · THE FOUNDATION OF THE CHURCH
THE ISSUE OF ETERNITY
CLEARLY, ORIGINALLY AND POWERFULLY OPENED

The basis · The righteousness of the law
The righteousness of God · The atonement · Justification
Traditional views considered · Righteousness imputed to faith
Faith counted for righteousness · Justification by Faith

'And it came to pass, when Jesus had ended these sayings, the people were astonished at his doctrine: for he taught them as one having authority, and not as the scribes.' Matthew 7:28,29.

Price £7.50 *(postage extra)*
Hardback 375 pages
Laminated bookjacket
ISBN 1870039 11 4

THE CHURCH: WHAT IS IT?

THE APOSTOLIC FOUNDATION
OF THE
CHRISTIAN CHURCH

Volume VII

The answer to this question proceeds first from the lips of Jesus himself, Mt. 16:18, later to be expounded by the words of the apostles whom he sent.

Neither fear of man nor favour from the world remotely affect the answer.

Here is the truth, the whole truth, and nothing but the truth.

The complete originality, the vast range, and the total fearlessness of this book command the attention in a way that is unique.

Read this book: you will never read another like it.

Outspokenly devastating yet devastatingly constructive.

OTHER TITLES

NOAH AND THE FLOOD

Noah and the Flood expounds with vital urgency the man and the message that heralded the end of the old world. The description of the flood itself is vividly realistic. The whole work has an unmistakable ring of authority, and speaks as 'Thus saith the Lord'.

'Mr. Metcalfe makes a skilful use of persuasive eloquence as he challenges the reality of one's profession of faith ... he gives a rousing call to a searching self-examination and evaluation of one's spiritual experience.'

The Monthly Record of the Free Church of Scotland.

Price £1.90 *(postage extra)*
(Laminated Cover)
ISBN 1 870039 22 X

DIVINE FOOTSTEPS

Divine Footsteps traces the pathway of the feet of the Son of man from the very beginning in the prophetic figures of the true in the old testament through the reality in the new; doing so in a way of experimental spirituality. At the last a glimpse of the coming glory is beheld as his feet are viewed as standing at the latter day upon the earth.

Price 95p *(postage extra)*
(Laminated Cover)
ISBN 1 870039 21 1

THE RED HEIFER

The Red Heifer was the name given to a sacrifice used by the children of Israel in the Old Testament—as recorded in Numbers 19—in which a heifer was slain and burned. Cedar wood, hyssop and scarlet were cast into the burning, and the ashes were mingled with running water and put in a vessel. It was kept for the children of Israel for a water of separation: it was a purification for sin.

In this unusual book the sacrifice is brought up to date and its relevance to the church today is shown.

Price 75p *(postage extra)*
ISBN 0 9502515 4 2

THE WELLS OF SALVATION

The Wells of Salvation is written from a series of seven powerful addresses preached at Tylers Green. It is a forthright and experimental exposition of Isaiah 12:3, 'Therefore with joy shall ye draw water out of the wells of salvation.'

Price £1.50 *(postage extra)*
(Laminated Cover)
ISBN 0 9502515 6 9

OF GOD OR MAN?

LIGHT FROM GALATIANS

The Epistle to the Galatians contends for deliverance from the law and from carnal ministry.

The Apostle opens his matter in two ways:

Firstly, Paul vindicates himself and his ministry against those that came not from God above, but from Jerusalem below.

Secondly, he defends the Gospel and evangelical liberty against legal perversions and bondage to the flesh.

Price £1.45 *(postage extra)*
(Laminated Cover)
ISBN 0 9506366 3 0

A QUESTION FOR POPE JOHN PAUL II

As a consequence of his many years spent apart in prayer, lonely vigil, and painstaking study of the scripture, John Metcalfe asks a question and looks for an answer from Pope John Paul II.

Price £1.25. *(postage extra)*
(Laminated Cover)
ISBN 0 9506366 4 9

THE BOOK OF RUTH

The Book of Ruth is set against the farming background of old testament Israel at the time of the Judges, the narrative—unfolding the work of God in redemption—being marked by a series of agricultural events.

These events—the famine; the barley harvest; the wheat harvest; the winnowing—possessed a hidden spiritual significance to that community, but, much more, they speak in figure directly to our own times, as the book reveals.

Equally contemporary appear the characters of Ruth, Naomi, Boaz, and the first kinsman, drawn with spiritual perception greatly to the profit of the reader.

Price £4.95 *(postage extra)*
Hardback 200 pages
Laminated bookjacket
ISBN 1 870039 17 3

'TRACT FOR THE TIMES' SERIES

THE GOSPEL OF GOD

'TRACT FOR THE TIMES' SERIES

The Gospel of God. Beautifully designed, this tract positively describes the gospel under the following headings: The Gospel is of God; The Gospel is Entirely of God; The Gospel is Entire in Itself; The Gospel is Preached; The Gospel Imparts Christ; and, Nothing But the Gospel Imparts Christ.

Price 25p *(postage extra)*
(Laminated Cover)
No. 1 in the Series

THE STRAIT GATE

'TRACT FOR THE TIMES' SERIES

The Strait Gate. Exceptionally well made, this booklet consists of extracts from 'The Messiah', compiled in such a way as to challenge the shallowness of much of today's 'easy-believism', whilst positively pointing to the strait gate.

Price 25p *(postage extra)*
(Laminated Cover)
No. 2 in the Series

ETERNAL SONSHIP AND TAYLOR BRETHREN

'TRACT FOR THE TIMES' SERIES

Eternal Sonship and Taylor Brethren. This booklet is highly recommended, particularly for those perplexed by James Taylor's teaching against the eternal sonship of Christ.

Price 25p *(postage extra)*
(Laminated Cover)
No. 3 in the Series

MARKS OF THE NEW TESTAMENT CHURCH

'TRACT FOR THE TIMES' SERIES

Marks of the New Testament Church. This exposition from Acts 2:42 declares what were, and what were not, the abiding marks of the church. The apostles' doctrine, fellowship and ordinances are lucidly explained.

Price 25p *(postage extra)*
(Laminated Cover)
No. 4 in the Series

THE CHARISMATIC DELUSION

'TRACT FOR THE TIMES' SERIES

The Charismatic Delusion. A prophetic message revealing the fundamental error of this movement which has swept away so many in the tide of its popularity. Here the delusion is dispelled.

Price 25p *(postage extra)*
(Laminated Cover)
No. 5 in the Series

PREMILLENNIALISM EXPOSED

'TRACT FOR THE TIMES' SERIES

Premillennialism Exposed. Well received evangelically, particularly through the influence of J.N. Darby, the Schofield bible, and the Plymouth Brethren, Premillennialism has assumed the cloak of orthodoxy. In this tract the cloak is removed, and the unorthodoxy of this system is exposed. A remarkable revelation.

Price 25p *(postage extra)*
(Laminated Cover)
No. 6 in the Series

JUSTIFICATION AND PEACE

'TRACT FOR THE TIMES' SERIES

Justification and Peace. This tract is taken from a message preached in December 1984 at Penang Hill, Malaysia. In this well-known address, peace with God is seen to be based upon nothing save justification by faith. No one should miss this tract.

Price 25p *(postage extra)*
(Laminated Cover)
No. 7 in the Series

FAITH OR PRESUMPTION?

'TRACT FOR THE TIMES' SERIES

Faith or presumption? The eighth tract in this vital series exposes the difference between faith and presumption, showing that faith is not of the law, neither is is apart from the work of God, nor is it of man. The work of God in man that precedes saving faith is opened generally and particularly, and the tract goes on to reveal positively the nature of saving faith. Belief and 'easy-believism' are contrasted, making clear the difference between the two, as the system of presumption—called easy-believism—is clearly shown, and the way of true belief pointed out with lucid clarity.

Price 25p *(postage extra)*
(Laminated Cover)
No. 8 in the Series

THE ELECT UNDECEIVED

'TRACT FOR THE TIMES' SERIES

The Elect undeceived, the ninth Tract for the Times, earnestly contends for 'the faith once delivered to the saints' in a way that is spiritually edifying, positive, and subject to the Lord Jesus Christ according to the scriptures.

The Tract is a response to the pamphlet 'Salvation and the Church' published jointly by the Catholic Truth Society and Church House Publishing, in which the Anglican and Roman Catholic Commissioners agree together about JUSTIFICATION. The pamphlet shows how they have agreed.

Price 25p *(postage extra)*
(Laminated Cover)
No. 9 in the Series

JUSTIFYING RIGHTEOUSNESS

'TRACT FOR THE TIMES' SERIES

Justifying Righteousness. Was it wrought by the law of Moses or by the blood of Christ? Written not in the language of dead theology but that of the living God, here is the vital and experimental doctrine of the new testament. Part of the book 'Justification by Faith', nevertheless this tract has a message in itself essential to those who would know and understand the truth.

Price 25p *(postage extra)*
(Laminated Cover)
No. 10 in the Series

RIGHTEOUSNESS IMPUTED

'TRACT FOR THE TIMES' SERIES

Righteousness Imputed. The truth of the gospel and the fallacy of tradition. Here the gospel trumpet of the jubilee is sounded in no uncertain terms, as on the one hand that truth essential to be believed for salvation is opened from holy scripture, and on the other the errors of Brethrenism are brought to light in a unique and enlightening way. This tract is taken from the book 'Justification by Faith', but in itself it conveys a message of great penetration and clarity.

Price 25p *(postage extra)*
(Laminated Cover)
No. 11 in the Series

THE GREAT DECEPTION

'TRACT FOR THE TIMES' SERIES

The Great Deception. The erosion of Justification by faith. All ministers, every Christian, and each assembly ought not only to possess but to read and reread this prophetic message as the word of the Lord to this generation, set in the context of the age. This tract is part of the book 'Justification by Faith' but contains within itself a message which is at once vital and authoritative.

Price 25p *(postage extra)*
(Laminated Cover)
No. 12 in the Series

A FAMINE IN THE LAND

'TRACT FOR THE TIMES' SERIES

A Famine in the Land. Taken from the Book of Ruth, with telling forcefulness this tract opens conditions exactly parallel to those of our own times. 'Behold, the days come, saith the Lord God, that I will send a famine in the land, not a famine of bread, nor a thirst for water, but of hearing the words of the Lord: and they shall wander from sea to sea, and from the north even to the east, they shall run to and fro to seek the word of the Lord, and shall not find it.'

Price 25p *(postage extra)*
(Laminated Cover)
No. 13 in the Series

BLOOD AND WATER

'TRACT FOR THE TIMES' SERIES

Blood and Water. Of the four gospels, only John reveals the truth that blood was shed at the cross. When it was shed, Jesus was dead already. With the blood there came forth water. But what do these things mean? With devastating present-day application, this tract tells you what they mean.

Price 25p *(postage extra)*
(Laminated Cover)
No. 14 in the Series

WOMEN BISHOPS?

'TRACT FOR THE TIMES' SERIES

Women Bishops? This is a question that has arisen in America, but should it have arisen at all?

Read this tract and find out the authoritative answer.

Price 25p *(postage extra)*
(Laminated Cover)
No. 15 in the Series

THE HEAVENLY VISION

'TRACT FOR THE TIMES' SERIES

The Heavenly Vision not only transformed the prophet himself, it became a savour of life unto life—or death unto death—to all the people.

'*Where there is no vision the people perish*', Proverbs 29:18. This is true. But where is the vision today? And what is the vision today? This tract answers those questions.

Price 25p *(Postage extra)*
(Laminated Cover)
No. 16 in the Series

EVANGELICAL TRACTS

EVANGELICAL TRACTS

1. **The Two Prayers of Elijah.** Green card cover, price 10p.

2. **Wounded for our Transgressions.** Gold card cover, price 10p.

3. **The Blood of Sprinkling.** Red card cover, price 10p.

4. **The Grace of God that brings Salvation.** Blue card cover, price 10p.

5. **The Name of Jesus.** Rose card cover, price 10p.

6. **The Ministry of the New Testament.** Purple card cover, price 10p.

7. **The Death of the Righteous** (*The closing days of J.B. Stoney*) by A.M.S. (his daughter). Ivory card cover, Price 10p.

ECCLESIA TRACTS

ECCLESIA TRACTS

NEWLY PUBLISHED

The Beginning of the Ecclesia by John Metcalfe. No. 1 in the Series, Sand grain cover, Price 10p.

Churches and the Church by J.N. Darby. Edited. No. 2 in the Series, Sand grain cover, Price 10p.

The Ministers of Christ by John Metcalfe. No. 3 in the Series, Sand grain cover, Price 10p.

The Inward Witness by George Fox. Edited. No. 4 in the Series, Sand grain cover, Price 10p.

The Notion of a Clergyman by J.N. Darby. Edited. No. 5 in the Series, Sand grain cover, Price 10p.

The Servant of the Lord by William Huntington. Edited and Abridged. No. 6 in the Series, Sand grain cover, Price 10p.

One Spirit by William Kelly. Edited. No. 7 in the Series, Sand grain cover, Price 10p.

The Funeral of Arminianism by William Huntington. Edited and Abridged. No. 8 in the Series, Sand grain cover, Price 10p.

One Body by William Kelly. Edited. No. 9 in the Series, Sand grain cover, Price 10p.

False Churches and True by John Metcalfe. No. 10 in the Series, Sand grain cover, Price 10p.

Separation from Evil by J.N. Darby. Edited. No. 11 in the Series, Sand grain cover, Price 10p.

The Remnant by J.B. Stoney. Edited. No. 12 in the Series, Sand grain cover, Price 10p.

MINISTRY BY JOHN METCALFE

TAPE MINISTRY BY JOHN METCALFE
FROM ENGLAND AND THE FAR EAST
IS AVAILABLE.

In order to obtain this free recorded ministry, please send your blank cassette (C.90) and the cost of the return postage, including your name and address in block capitals, to the John Metcalfe Publishing Trust, Church Road, Tylers Green, Penn, Bucks, HP10 8LN. Tapelists are available on request.

Owing to the increased demand for the tape ministry, we are unable to supply more than two tapes per order, except in the case of meetings for the hearing of tapes, where a special arrangement can be made.

THE MINISTRY OF THE NEW TESTAMENT

The purpose of this substantial A4 gloss paper magazine is to provide spiritual and experimental ministry with sound doctrine which rightly and prophetically divides the Word of Truth.

Readers of our books will already know the high standards of our publications. They can be confident that these pages will maintain that quality, by giving access to enduring ministry from the past, much of which is derived from sources that are virtually unobtainable today, and publishing a living ministry from the present. Selected articles from the following writers have already been included:

ELI ASHDOWN · ABRAHAM BOOTH · JOHN BUNYAN
JOHN BURGON · JOHN CALVIN · DONALD CARGILL
JOHN CENNICK · J.N. DARBY · GEORGE FOX · JOHN FOXE
WILLIAM GADSBY · WILLIAM HUNTINGTON · WILLIAM KELLY
JOHN KENNEDY · JOHN KERSHAW · HANSERD KNOLLYS
JAMES LEWIS · MARTIN LUTHER · ROBERT MURRAY MCCHEYNE
JOHN METCALFE · ALEXANDER—SANDY—PEDEN
J.C. PHILPOT · JAMES RENWICK · J.B. STONEY
HENRY TANNER · JOHN VINALL · JOHN WARBURTON
JOHN WELWOOD · GEORGE WHITEFIELD · J.A. WYLIE

Price £1.75 *(postage included)*
Issued Spring, Summer, Autumn, Winter.

Book Order Form

Please send to the address below:-

		Price	Quantity
A Question for Pope John Paul II		£1.25	......
Of God or Man?		£1.45	......
Noah and the Flood		£1.90	......
Divine Footsteps		£0.95	......
The Red Heifer		£0.75	......
The Wells of Salvation		£1.50	......
The Book of Ruth (Hardback edition)		£4.95	......
Divine Meditations of William Huntington		£2.35	......
Present-Day Conversions of the New Testament Kind		£2.25	......
Psalms, Hymns & Spiritual Songs (Hardback edition)			
The Psalms of the Old Testament		£2.50	......
Spiritual Songs from the Gospels		£2.50	......
The Hymns of the New Testament		£2.50	......
'Apostolic Foundation of the Christian Church' series			
Foundations Uncovered	Vol.I	£0.30	......
The Birth of Jesus Christ	Vol.II	£0.95	......
The Messiah	Vol.III	£2.45	......
The Son of God and Seed of David (Hardback edition)	Vol.IV	£6.95	......
Christ Crucified (Hardback edition)	Vol.V	£6.95	......
Justification by Faith (Hardback edition)	Vol.VI	£7.50	......
The Church: What is it? (Hardback edition)	Vol.VII	£7.75	......

Name and Address (in block capitals)

. . . .

. . . .

. . . .

If money is sent with order please allow for postage. Please address to:- The John Metcalfe Publishing Trust, Church Road, Tylers Green, Penn, Bucks, HP10 8LN.

Tract Order Form

Please send to the address below:-

	No.	Price	Quantity
Evangelical Tracts			
The Two Prayers of Elijah		£0.10	......
Wounded for our Transgressions		£0.10	......
The Blood of Sprinkling		£0.10	......
The Grace of God that Brings Salvation		£0.10	......
The Name of Jesus		£0.10	......
The Ministry of the New Testament		£0.10	......
The Death of the Righteous by A.M.S.		£0.10	......
'Tract for the Times' series			
The Gospel of God	No.1	£0.25	......
The Strait Gate	No.2	£0.25	......
Eternal Sonship and Taylor Brethren	No.3	£0.25	......
Marks of the New Testament Church	No.4	£0.25	......
The Charismatic Delusion	No.5	£0.25	......
Premillennialism Exposed	No.6	£0.25	......
Justification and Peace	No.7	£0.25	......
Faith or presumption?	No.8	£0.25	......
The Elect undeceived	No.9	£0.25	......
Justifying Righteousness	No.10	£0.25	......
Righteousness Imputed	No.11	£0.25	......
The Great Deception	No.12	£0.25	......
A Famine in the Land	No.13	£0.25	......
Blood and Water	No.14	£0.25	......
Women Bishops?	No.15	£0.25	......
The Heavenly Vision	No.16	£0.25	......
Ecclesia Tracts			
The Beginning of the Ecclesia	No.1	£0.10	......
Churches and the Church (J.N.D.)	No.2	£0.10	......
The Ministers of Christ	No.3	£0.10	......
The Inward Witness (G.F.)	No.4	£0.10	......
The Notion of a Clergyman (J.N.D.)	No.5	£0.10	......
The Servant of the Lord (W.H.)	No.6	£0.10	......
One Spirit (W.K.)	No.7	£0.10	......
The Funeral of Arminianism (W.H.)	No.8	£0.10	......
One Body (W.K.)	No.9	£0.10	......
False Churches and True	No.10	£0.10	......
Separation from Evil (J.N.D.)	No.11	£0.10	......
The Remnant (J.B.S.)	No.12	£0.10	......

Name and Address (in block capitals)

. . . .

. . . .

. . . .

If money is sent with order please allow for postage. Please address to:- The John Metcalfe Publishing Trust, Church Road, Tylers Green, Penn, Bucks, HP10 8LN.

Magazine Order Form

Name and Address (in block capitals)

. . . .

. . . .

. . . .

Please send me .... current copy/copies of The Ministry of the New Testament.

Please send me .... year/s subscription.

I enclose a cheque/postal order for £ ....

(Price: including postage, U.K. £1.75; Overseas £1.90)
(One year's subscription: Including postage, U.K. £7.00; Overseas £7.60)

Cheques should be made payable to The John Metcalfe Publishing Trust, and for overseas subscribers should be in pounds sterling drawn on a London Bank.

10 or more copies to one address will qualify for a 10% discount

Back numbers from Spring 1986 available.

Please send to The John Metcalfe Publishing Trust, Church Road, Tylers Green, Penn, Bucks, HP10 8LN

All Publications of the Trust are subsidised by the Publishers.